How to Feed Your Family for £5.00 a Day

Bernadine Lawrence

D0188530

Thorsons

An Imprint of HarperCollins*Publishers*

Thorsons
An Imprint of HarperCollins*Publishers*
77–85 Fulham Palace Road,
Hammersmith, London W6 8JB

First published by Thorsons
as *How to Feed Your Family for £4.00 a Day* 1989
This revised edition published 1991
3   5   7   9   10   8   6   4

Bernadine Lawrence asserts the moral right to
be identified as the author of this work

A catalogue record for this book
is available from the British Library

ISBN 0 7225 2571 0

Typeset by Burns & Smith Ltd., Derby
Printed in Great Britain by
HarperCollinsManufacturing Glasgow

How to Feed Your Family for £5.00 a Day

Bernadine Lawrence was born in Dominica in the West Indies, but has lived in England since she was a child. After training as a dancer she worked internationally in cabaret, and in London with the African Dance Theatre.

Creativity of another sort took priority however when she gave birth to her first child (the first of four). Adjusting to a lower income, she began to 'spin gold out of straw', conjuring up delicious and nutritious meals out of the most basic ingredients. Her recipes follow the 'perfect diet' now recommended by the World Health Organisation, which Bernadine believes has played a great part in maintaining her youth and agility in her new role — teaching exercise to music.

Contents

Dedication

To Naughty Ned and Cuddly Cath, two of London's loveliest greengrocers.

Foreword

In the autumn of 1986 a letter to *The Times* aroused my interest. It described how at least one family, living in a high-rise council flat in an expensive part of London, ate well and healthily on supplementary benefit. I was in touch with Bernadine Lawrence at once.

Her idea of a book to help those in a similar position to her own family had not been well received by the groups dedicated to helping those caught in the poverty trap because they thought it might be used to depress the benefit and that is definitely not why this book was written. It is written with the principle in mind that a caring society should look after those who, through no fault of their own, are unable to be breadwinners.

How to Feed Your Family for £5.00 a Day is more, far more than a guide on how to eat cheaply. It is a return to basic good food made from the basic raw materials that so many have forgotten — or never been taught — how to use. It is the triumph of intelligent common sense over the problems of living on a low income.

In this book, Bernadine has reversed the trend towards highly packaged convenience foods that don't actually taste all that good or do you much good either and gone back to basics with, for example, the marvellous nutritive value of her splendid wholemeal loaf — a mainstay of the sound and economical nutrition of the Lawrence household, which comprises mum and dad plus four happy, healthy children aged between 15 months and 13 years.

Making just two meals for a family of four, you will recover the cost of the book and, from then on, you will profit both by saving money and through better health. *How to Feed Your Family for £5.00 a Day* should be in every home and I wish it every success.

MAURICE HANSSEN

Foreword

When I called on Bernie Lawrence and her young family she was busy preparing a basket of fresh, home-cooked food for the children to take to the local Harvest Festival. Not for Bernie the traditional urban offering of a tin of rice pudding and a box of biscuits. She can't afford such things.

Although she has the advantage of living in fashionable Chelsea in a council flat overlooking the Thames that would fetch half a million if it were 'gentrified', Bernie is financially highly disadvantaged. Her sole income is a handout from the State and after paying for essentials, there's not much left over on which to feed six people healthily. She knew from experience that there wasn't much good health in costly packets and tins and heavily advertised 'convenience' foods. In any case, there wasn't enough money in her purse for that kind of stuff; every penny had to be made to count nutritionally.

Bernie's great achievement in feeding the family on £5 a day demonstrates that there *is* life beyond white sliced bread, frozen burgers, oven-fried chips and toffees. Bernie may be bobbing about on the poverty line but she has no intention of drowning.

Over the years she has devised a wide repertoire of meals which cost very little, are simple to prepare and full of goodness. This is healthy food, full of taste and flavour. It may be cheap but it's very, very cheerful. The recipes in *How to Feed Your Family for £5.00 a Day* are a survival manual for those caught in the poverty trap. But the book is more than that — if gastronomy means an intelligent and creative use of the best raw materials at your disposal then this is a distinguished exercise in gastronomy and triumphant proof that the art of eating well can be the prerogative of the poor as well as the well-heeled.

DEREK COOPER

Introduction

Ten years ago I had to dismiss my chauffeur and sell my Bentley after a failed business venture. Often it is the loss of a status symbol which causes shame and a feeling of worthlessness.

But it can mean the start of a new venture in life, the beginning of self-discovery where you find you have to get your priorities sorted out and when hidden strengths and talents start to emerge out of necessity. Necessity *is* the mother of invention. Business failure can sometimes be a blessing in disguise.

I was used to spending £150 a week on food, drawing up outside restaurants, buying lots of take-aways and my bread from specialist food shops. After my income dropped dramatically I had to learn very quickly how to manage on a pittance. I was fearful of the future and dreaded those quarterly bills. I just did not see how I could possibly manage, and at first couldn't — I was sinking quickly into debt and even running out of food at the end of the week.

In order to manage I allowed myself just £4 a day to feed my family and buy household goods. I started cooking and experimenting with ingredients, trying to reproduce many of the meals I had enjoyed in vegetarian restaurants and found I could produce delicious meals which were nutritionally excellent and cost very little. So we were eating a superior diet at minimum cost, thus enabling us to direct our resources elsewhere — we do not live to eat, we eat to live.

As the number of my recipes grew we found we were actually eating better than ever and had discovered the perfect diet — the very kind now recommended by the World Health Organization (WHO), and it was ecologically sound and incredibly cheap; literally, it did not cost the earth!

And now, ten years after, I can fully appreciate the rewards of this diet — the accumulative effect is tremendous. I feel at a peak of physical fitness — fit for life, with all its many varied and often conflicting demands, here towards the 21st century where only the fittest survive.

Recently I was delighted to learn in a lecture given by a nutritionist specializing in exercise and sports nutrition, that I was eating my way to optimum physical and mental fitness. My high carbohydrate diet consisting of fresh fruits and vegetables, whole grains and cereals, peas, beans and lentils is five-star fuel for the body — the body is a machine; if you don't use it you lose it, and if you don't give it the correct fuel it is liable to break down.

And as for losing weight — weight watchers watch out! Stop watching your weight! You only slow down your metabolic rate anyway when you drastically reduce your intake of food, and when you start eating normally again you just put on weight (a method often used to fatten pigs). Just three regular meals of the type to be found in this book is all a body needs a day, and I think I owe my lovely slim figure to my high fibre, high carbohydrate diet.

The disease prevalent in this society of being overfed and undernourished is due to the popularity of highly refined foods. But on a high fibre diet one can occasionally eat fish and chips, cakes and so on without worry; it is only when one's overall diet consists mainly of refined foods that one falls prey to obesity, heart disease and all the illnesses associated with poor nutrition.

Children also thrive on this diet — my children certainly do, and love it. Yet child poverty is growing in Great Britain and the spectre of Tiny Tim is still with us. Just a nominal amount of information could transform these children's lives and send them to bed happily with full bellies.

Indeed, I've received poignant letters from parents who have been at their wits' end wondering what to feed the kids with 'just odds and ends in the cupboard' thanking me deeply — everytime I make your bread I get really big-headed because I feel so proud of myself and my children love it' (*real* mother's pride).

Just one such letter confirms the very real and urgent need for the valuable information in this book. Yet there are various individuals, organizations, charities and politicians to the left and right of the political spectrum who have a vested interest in keeping people ignorant. It is not for nothing that British supermarkets are the most profitable in the world. And until people are given this information they literally do not have a choice; they remain fodder to the mass media and the junk food giants and are denied the most basic of freedoms — knowledge on how to look after oneself.

But ignorance about nutrition is widespread at all levels of society. It is not just the poor who are devoid of knowledge. You don't have to be wealthy to eat healthily, and the reverse is true — many wealthy people are unhealthy because of their bad eating habits.

So if you want to eat your way to perfect health follow the recipes in this book — just good, down-to-earth, common-sense, simple and wholesome meals.

1
Basic Essentials

Items contained in this section are either whole recipes which will prove very useful in keeping your diet both cheap and healthy or preparations which you will find essential when making many of the other recipes throughout the Benefit Book and, lastly, one utility which I have found crucial in preparation of many of those recipes.

Note on Measuring

The most accurate way of measuring with a spoon is to use level measures, that is, level off to the top of the spoon with a knife. (A heaped spoon can contain anything from two to four times as much as a level spoon.)

A pinch = $\frac{1}{4}$ teaspoon
2 teaspoons = 1 dessertspoon
2 dessertspoons = 1 tablespoon
25g/1oz flour = 1 heaped tablespoon
25g/1oz sugar = 1 level tablespoon

In our household we prefer to measure ingredients using cups. Conveniently, one of our cups holds 285ml/$\frac{1}{2}$ pint of liquid, thus a measuring jug, filled to the 285ml/$\frac{1}{2}$ pint mark, can serve ideally when measuring out cupfuls. For those of you who feel that cup measurements would be a lot easier to use, I have listed below some of the staple ingredients used in this book and their amounts per cup.

Beans — 1cup = 165g/5½ oz
Cornmeal — 1 cup = 140g/5 oz
Flour — 1 cup = 115g/4 oz
Lentils — 1 cup = 165g/5½ oz
Macaroni — 1 cup = 140g/5 oz
Milk powder — 1 cup = 115g/4 oz
Porridge oats — 1 cup = 115g/4 oz
Raisins — 1 cup = 140g/5 oz
Rice — 1 cup = 165g/5½ oz
  Cooked — 1 cup = 170g/6 oz
Rolled oats — 1 cup = 115g/4 oz
Sugar — 1 cup = 170g/6 oz
Sultanas — 1 cup = 140g/5 oz

In fact, any need for such elaborate machinery as weighing scales (the dread of many a non-cook) can be avoided altogether simply by taking note of the quantities in which foods are bought and dividing them appropriately. For example, when making a pastry case for a Quick Quiche simply cut half (or just under half) off a 250g/9 oz block of margarine, and when making Bargain Bread use all but one-tenth of a 1.5kg/3lb 5 oz bag of wholemeal flour, and the only instruments required are a knife and a bowl.

A Note About Shopping

The costs given in this book for recipes should be taken as approximates, of course, but are based upon the prices I pay in Chelsea — a locality not exactly well known for low prices with one of the highest concentrations of millionaires in the land. Thus, if it's possible in Chelsea it should be possible anywhere.

I am quite fortunate in that my local greengrocer on Cheyne Walk, who also caters for Paul Getty, has very reasonable prices because he always gets to market and back by 4 am in all weathers, come rain, snow or hurricane (hence his nickname — Hurricane Ned), and that way secures the bargains of the day.

I favour a well known supermarket, on the Kings Road, where you can be sure of good customer service and bargains such as home-produced Cheddar at £1.15 a pound. It is there where I purchase my flour, oats, pulses, lentils etc. You don't have to go to a health food shop to buy brown rice and blackeye beans — it's much cheaper to shop in a supermarket that has its own 'Home Brands'.

The only time I bother going to a health food shop is when I buy my dried yeast. I buy a large container — 500g for £2.35. This is four times the size of the one sold in the supermarket and lasts 8–12 weeks when baking on a regular basis. If you have a small container of yeast (125g) simply fill it from the large container: that way the yeast will stay fresher in the large one.

Also, if you like, every time you have to refill the small container you can just deduct 59p from the 'shopping purse' (see below) rather than pay for the yeast in one go.

An important tip to remember is to keep a 'shopping purse', that is, a purse used strictly for your weekly groceries. Say, you want to allow yourself £33 for the week, put that amount in your purse at the beginning of the week. That way you can easily tell if you are keeping within budget.

Should you overshoot your weekly target in the beginning, this need not mean a failure to budget successfully. If, for example, in the first week you should decide on Mulligatawny Soup for Wednesday's lunch, which means buying a pack of cayenne pepper for 50p, only to use $\frac{1}{2}$ a penny's worth, you'll not need to buy any more for a month of Sundays, and your weekly budget will gradually balance out.

A good way to keep within budget is to use up any ingredients you may already have in. For example, if you have plenty of carrots, lettuce, tomato and cucumber and about $\frac{1}{2}$lb of lentils, you could make a Lentil Flan. You would only need to buy onions, garlic, lemon, watercress and potatoes to make Lentil Flan with baked potatoes and Simple Salad. This method is particularly useful towards the end of the week when you can use up ingredients in soups and stews etc.

In this new edition we have decided that it is not necessary to cost every single ingredient and have just given the total price for a recipe. The prices in the exemplary shopping list below should serve as a good guideline. It is a genuine shopping list of mine and feeds well my family of 6, though generally the recipes in this book are for four adults.

With inflation, the scourge of every household, still effectively unchecked you may find items on your shop shelves soon costing more, but this will do nothing, in effect, to erode the relative value of your book — for even if costs were to double overnight taking your weekly food bill to £70, that would be far less than if your former bill had been, say, £50 per week thus increasing to £100.

Tips for Buying for One or Two

Obviously single people and couples can make great use of this book. Many students, aware of the fact that lentils and pulses contain more protein than prime lean beef at just one sixteenth of the price, are already experimenting with these ingredients.

Most of the ingredients in the recipes can be divided more or less by two, and surpluses can be chilled or frozen for future use. For example, a couple need only bake one large loaf which should last two days. This is kept fresh, when cooled, in a plastic bag. Either half a bag of flour (1½lbs) can be used or the surplus dough kept in the fridge for 2–3 days, after which it can be allowed to rise in a warm oven for slightly longer before baking.

Single people may also find it convenient to bake 1 large wholemeal loaf, which can be transformed into a quick wholesome meal of baked beans on toast or bread and cheese pudding, or simply served with quick soups and stews.

It is not advisable to buy large quantities of highly perishable foods. These should be bought daily or every other day.

Storing food

Chilled food should be put into a fridge as soon as it is cool; don't wait for it to get cold.

Cool food as quickly as possible but don't put it in the fridge whilst hot or it will warm up the other food.

Don't keep warming up food and cooling it down — if you make a big stew, for example, heat what you need for each meal.

Reheated food should be cooked thoroughly for approximately 20 minutes.

Don't store cooked food in a fridge for more than three days.

A note about dietary supplements

As for dietary supplements, such as multivitamin pills, these are strictly unnecessary with the wholesome diet offered in this book. You need to eat well, anyway, to absorb these pills as water-based pills often pass straight through the body. Also, it is easy to overdose on vitamins A and D which then have toxic side-effects. Even non-red meat eaters need not supplement their diet with vitamin B12 as this can be found in eggs, milk, cheese, poultry and soya beans.

A Typical Weekly Shopping List

1 chicken	£3.00
2 bags wholemeal flour	£1.44
1 bag plain white flour	69
large tin baked beans	49
1 tin tomatoes	28
1kg porridge oats	59
500g raisins	75
500g red split lentils	55
500g wholewheat spaghetti	59
500g blackeye beans	65
2 × 500g sunflower margarine	£1.32
1 litre vegetable oil	65
2 tins pilchards	68
jar yeast extract	70

4 oz humous	55
1½lbs Cheddar	£1.73
2 mackerel	£1.60
1 kg frozen peas	74
8 oz coffee with chicory	95
7 pints milk (milk token)	
4 pints milk	£1.18
1 litre apple juice concentrate	£3.00
12 eggs	£1.10
1lb bag bacon pieces	£1.05
12 oz lamb's kidneys	95
9lb potatoes	£1.08
1 small red cabbage	30
3lb onions	60
1lb carrots	20
1lb sprouts	30
2lb apples	80
1lb pears	40
1 stick celery	40
10 oranges	£1.00
bunch bananas	60
1 green pepper	30
garlic	30
4 oz mushrooms	25
1 cucumber	50
1 lemon	10
3 lettuces	90
3 bunches watercress	90
1lb tomatoes	60
Total	£34.84

Bargain Bread

Baking your own bread! The idea no doubt sounds far-fetched, impractical, possible for some others, perhaps, but not for yourself. But if you consider that it takes only 20 minutes (yes 20!) to prepare 2 large wholemeal loaves (10 minutes per loaf) for around 39p each. That is probably less time than many of you are now willing to spend making an excursion, in all weathers, to pay twice as much for a grossly defective product handled by who knows how many and never with the same care as one's own bread. Is the idea really all that far-fetched when one discovers just how quick and easy a process making wholemeal bread is? All that seems far-fetched is that so few people do so.

Your family will love it and love you for it. Not only does baking one's own wholemeal bread increase the bread in your shopping purse and the nourishment in your diet, but your own morale will rise every time, along with the dough in your oven. My own loaves have brought some most touching compliments and from a wide assortment of people ranging from fellow-claimants to somebody with a bank balance nine figures long.

It is no coincidence that in our terminology money became increasingly referred to as dough or bread until the mass of people adopted these terms for common usage and they became forever woven into the language. Both these references have come about because of the significance of bread in our diet. Since time immemorial, from the instance that tribes chanted and prayed to their Gods to make their grain crops abundant so that they need never go short of bread, to the present when its very primacy still necessitates its inclusion in the Lord's Prayer, bread in all its many forms has been an important dietary staple for all nations. Technically speaking we have come a long way since say Roman Times but, paradoxically, their diet was superior to ours simply because the mass of people ate wholegrain bread. Our modern civilization has taken a huge step backwards in mass-producing bread stripped of its nutrients — the germ and the bran.

Grain is composed of three elements — the germ, the endosperm and the bran. The germ contains protein, thiamine, iron, riboflavin, niacin and vitamin E. The endosperm contains a little protein but is mainly carbohydrates. The bran is the protective coating around the grain and contains iron and B vitamins. Most people today in the West, in spite of the growing trend towards wholegrain bread still eat bread which contains little more than starch and it is impossible for the manufacturers to replace all the nutrients destroyed in the milling process. Bargain Bread is made from wholemeal flour and contains 100 per cent of the wheat grain. Not only is Bargain Bread high in fibre, it is also high in nourishment. This may be bread-line Britain, but this is bloody good bread!

For those of you catering for children the bread need not be entirely made from wholewheat flour. The very young and the elderly do not require as much fibre as the average adult, so it is perfectly all right to mix the flours.

I usually substitute 2–3 cups (8–12 ozs) of wholemeal flour approximately for the same amount of plain white flour, but there is nothing wrong with mixing the flours half and half and at times — say when you run out of wholemeal flour — to have a plain white loaf. Now that really is something else — a white loaf is usually enormous with a delicious crispy crust and is fine for children as long as they are eating plenty of fresh fruit and vegetables and receiving alternative wholegrains such as oats or brown rice, for example.

The same applies for the average adult — it's acceptable once in a while to eat plain white bread if you are basically on a high fibre diet including wholegrains, for we mustn't forget those B vitamins!

Of course mistakes can be made when baking one's own bread and such mistakes are most likely to occur in the initial attempts when you are least familiar with the routine. Therefore, hopefully, a brief reading of these guidelines prior to a first try at baking bread may help avert any of the three most common mistakes which might otherwise have had discouraging effects.

Firstly, in my own experience, the most common mistake has been to stand the yeast after mixing it to rise in an over-heated oven. Secondly, if the water used when mixing the yeast is too hot the result will be the same — the yeast will, in effect, be killed and will not rise (form a frothy head). If after some 10–15 minutes the yeast fails to rise it should be discarded for some fresh yeast; if it is not replaced then one is preparing 2 very heavy loaves destined not to rise. If, however, your yeast produces a fine head and is mixed successfully into a dough, then avoid the third and final downfall and do not stand the dough to rise in an over-warm oven, as this will have the same effect upon the yeast at this stage and your dough will not rise (expand) to produce large loaves.

But even if one of these mistakes is made at some point and the dough never rises, the outcome will just be smaller, heavier loaves which is only a cosmetic failure and in no way are such loaves deficient in terms of nourishment. So, on such occasions, I strongly recommend you to do as I have and consume such bread perhaps with a soup or in a bread and butter pudding, or simply cut into small cubes and served with warm milk and dried fruit and, of course, to try again!

Bargain Bread

Ingredients
850ml/1½ pints water
15ml/1 level tablespoon sugar
20ml/4 level teaspoons dried yeast (Allinson's)
1.4kg/3 lb wholemeal flour
10ml/2 level teaspoons salt

Method
1   Turn oven onto its lowest heat and leave to warm. Heat water until hand hot, slightly above blood heat (about 55°C/110°F). Dissolve the sugar in 60ml/4 tablespoons water, add the yeast and leave in a warm place to froth, 10 minutes approximately.
2   Grease and flour 2 large loaf tins. Measure flour and salt into a bowl. Add the yeast mixture then gradually add the rest of the water. Mix to a dough and knead for 10–15 minutes, adding more flour if necessary to make a dough that is smooth, elastic and not sticky. (With practice, the mixing bowl should be left quite clean.)
3   Halve the dough and place in the bread tins.
4   Switch off the oven and leave the dough inside for approximately 30 minutes or until the mixture has risen 2.5cm/1 inch above the rim of the tins.
5   Bake at 200°C/400°F (Gas Mark 6) for 40 minutes until brown on top.
6   Lastly, stand the loaves to cool on the wire rack from your grill. This will prevent them becoming too moist underneath.

Approximate cost of ingredients: 78p

- Bread — add a small amount of oil (1–2 table-spoons) to the dough to avoid too many crumbs when slicing. Alternatively, keep the bread crumbs for use in burgers and stuffings, etc.

Variations

Bread Buns

If short of suitable tins for making loaves, bread buns are quick and practical. Follow the recipe and method for Bargain Bread. Take half the kneaded dough and shape 10 bread buns. Place them on a greased baking sheet and leave them to rise in a warm place for 15–20 minutes or until they are twice their size. Bake on a low shelf of the oven for 25 minutes.

- Bread storage: when cool store bread in clean plastic bags tied tightly. This keeps the bread remarkably fresh.

Raisin Bread

Ingredients
30–45ml/2–3 level tablespoons brown sugar
850ml/1½ pints water (heated to 55°C/110°F)
30ml/6 teaspoons dried yeast
1.4kg/3 lb wholemeal flour
2.5ml/½ level teaspoon salt
275g/10 oz raisins
60ml/4 tablespoons vegetable oil (optional)
Optional egg wash of 1 egg beaten with 15ml/1 tablespoon
    brown sugar and 30ml/2 tablespoons milk

Method
1 Dissolve the sugar in 140ml/¼ pint of hot water, add
   yeast and leave to froth for 10 minutes.
2 Mix the flour, salt and raisins and pour into the yeast
   mixture. Knead and gradually add the rest of the water
   with the oil.
3 Continue as for Bargain Bread and if liked, brush the loaf
   with egg wash before baking.

Approximate cost of ingredients: £1.31

The Humble Spud

The humble spud, as we tend to think of it today, was not
always so humble. Only four centuries earlier and the potato
was quite a delicacy in Europe and grown only in the
gardens of the rich, having been fetched by Spaniards from
its homeland high in the Andes in South America where it
had long been cultivated. It tended to be eaten at rich and
privileged tables as a separate starter to meals, rather like
an avocado today.

But come the Industrial Revolution, the status of the potato changed as its potential to feed large numbers of people cheaply was realized until, by the middle of the eighteenth century, potatoes had replaced bread as the main foodstuff of more than half of the population. Methods of preparing the humble spud have, naturally, increased since then, some proving phenomenal (try to envisage Britain without all of its fish and chip shops or kids without potato crisps). But the demise of the humble spud in my view came with the advent of so-called instant mashed potatoes, when the vegetable was skinned and reduced to a colourless, flavourless pulp and sold in sachets bearing claims that the addition of measured volumes of boiling water would produce delicious mashed potatoes in seconds. I am still of the opinion that somebody ought to have challenged this claim under the Trade Descriptions Act.

Potatoes you will find, because of their potential for cheap nourishment, are an important component of many of my meals in the Benefit Book and are, therefore, indeed a Basic Essential but, despite this, I have no use for a potato peeler, the reason being that the removal of the skin from a potato would amount to the complete waste of a most beneficial part. This is because most of potato's fibre is in the skin and therefore, whether baking, boiling or roasting them, I use a small plastic pan-scrub to wash off excess dirt from any such vegetables. Then after scrubbing I remove any eyes or bad parts with a kitchen knife, retaining the maximum of the potato's fibre, calcium and vitamin C.

Baked Potatoes

Baking is by far my most frequent method of preparing potatoes. This is because (besides the fact I simply find baked potatoes delicious) I often use the oven to prepare the main part of the meal and a vacant top shelf inside will accommodate a large trayful of spuds and save the use of a top burner. This not only helps towards smaller gas bills but also reduces the chance of accidents in that often hectic pre-dinner period. The baked potato is also the humble spud cooked in its most wholesome form with none of the goodness lost in water which is then poured away.

Method
1   Simply wash each potato and remove any bad parts.
2   Bake on a top shelf at 200°C/400°F (Gas Mark 6) for 45 minutes.
3   Serve with margarine, salt and freshly ground black pepper.

A quick meal can be made by topping baked potatoes with grated cheese, baked beans or tuna and garnished with cucumber or tomatoes.

Roast Potatoes

Ingredients
900g/2 lb potatoes
85g/2 oz margarine or 45ml/2 tablespoons vegetable oil
Salt and freshly ground black pepper

Method
1 Wash, scrub and, if necessary, eye potatoes (remove any bad parts). Cut them in half and place them with fat in a baking tin (or around the roast) and roast them in a hot oven (220°C/425°F, Gas Mark 7) 45 minutes.
2 When they are partially cooked, turn them over so that they brown on both sides.
3 Season with salt and freshly ground pepper 5 minutes before serving.

Approximate cost: 27p

Boiled Potatoes

Ingredients
900g/2 lb new potatoes

Method
1 Scrub the potatoes lightly and chop them into halves or quarters, depending on their size.
2 Cook them in boiling, salted water for about 15 minutes until tender but firm. Drain and serve.
3 Alternatively cook with parsley, mint or chopped chives.

Approximate cost: 40p

Cheese Stuffed Potatoes

Ingredients
900g/2 lb potatoes
225g/8 oz grated Cheddar
85g/3 oz margarine or butter
Salt and freshly ground black pepper

Method
1   Wash, scrub, eye and stab potatoes. Place them in a hot oven (220°C/425°F/Gas Mark 7) on a baking tray or tin and bake for 45 minutes until cooked. (Test by inserting a fork to find out if they are tender inside.)
2   Remove potatoes from the oven and cut them in half. Scoop out the cooked potato, mash and combine with the cheese and margarine.
3   Season with salt and freshly ground black pepper and fill the potato cases with the mix. Return to the oven and continue to bake for 10–15 minutes until golden brown on top. Serve with salad etc.

Approximate cost: 99p

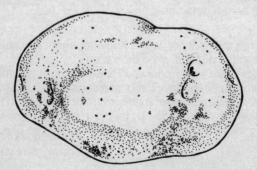

Creamed Potatoes

Ingredients
900g/2 lb potatoes
55g/2 oz margarine or butter
Salt and freshly ground black pepper

Method
1   Wash, scrub and eye potatoes. Chop them up small and boil for 10–15 minutes until tender.
2   Drain the potatoes, the mash them. Add the margarine and blend in thoroughly.
3   Season to taste with salt and freshly ground black pepper.

Approximate cost: 34p

Potato Fritters

Ingredients
900g/2 lb cooked potatoes, mashed
30ml/2 level tablespoons bread crumbs
5 eggs
10ml/2 level teaspoons tomato purée
Crushed garlic, to taste
45–60ml/3–4 tablespoons vegetable oil

Method
1   Mix all the ingredients and season with salt and freshly ground black pepper.
2   Shape into flat cakes and fry in a little oil until brown on both sides. Alternatively, brown in oven in an oiled tray.

Approximate cost: 75p

Saucy Potatoes

Ingredients
900g/2 lb potatoes
55–85g/2–3 oz streaky bacon, cubed
1 large onion, finely chopped
30ml/2 level tablespoons flour
570ml/1 pint milk
A little grated nutmeg

Method
1   Wash, scrub and eye the potatoes. Cut them in half and boil them until tender for about 15 minutes.
2   Drain and cut them into thick slices while they are still hot.
3   Return the potatoes to the pan, cover and keep them warm on the cooker.
4   Fry the bacon, add the onion and continue to cook until golden.
5   Add the flour and gradually add the milk. Stir well and bring to the boil.
6   Season with salt and pepper then combine the potatoes with the sauce. Stir and simmer together briefly. Serve hot.

Approximate cost of ingredients: 80p

Brown Rice

Brown rice is a Basic Essential in this book because it can be included in so many recipes and is an excellent source of roughage (fibre) and nutrients. The cultivation of brown rice and other grain crops which were easily grown, high-yielding and storable was a major event in the founding of modern civilization, for only with a dependable food supply readily available were countless tribes able to stop their wanderings in search of food, and settle down.

Brown rice is a still a Basic Essential for many people around the world, but highly milled and polished white rice is favoured in the West. Sadly, Third World countries are following suit and eating more white rice — a highly dangerous exercise for many dependant on rice who, as a result, develop Beri Beri (due to B vitamin loss) and die in their thousands.

Indeed, in many countries brown rice is left for the poor whilst the rich and fashionable eat white rice in adundance. This point was emphasized recently when speaking with a Malaysian friend. She happened to mention that she was on a diet and had cut out rice totally, a task which was particularly difficult, she stressed, as rice was a staple food in her country and formed the basis of many of her favourite meals.

'No, rice isn't fattening!' I declared (foolishly thinking she was referring to brown rice).

'It is!' she protested. Then when I started to extol the virtues of brown rice she screwed up her face. 'That's just for the poor people!' she exclaimed, and would not entertain the idea at all. Such is the social stigma of brown rice for many.

So here we have another paradox where the poor, who cannot afford the highly polished white rice, eat instead, brown rice which is far superior, whilst the rich and affluent who buy the highly esteemed white rice, eat an inferior produce.

White rice is grossly deficient because it has had the bran and the germ removed. The bran and the germ contain 80 per cent of the thiamine (vitamin B_1), whereas the endosperm, though constituting 90 per cent of the weight, contains less than 10 per cent of the thiamine. Also, research has shown that certain cardiac conditions and heart disease are related to thiamine deficiency — little wonder that heart disease is such a major killer in the West.

It is important to remember that rice washed in water too

thoroughly loses some of the B vitamins, which are dissolved out. Similarly, if rice is boiled in excess water a considerable proportion of the B vitamins are likely to be discarded in the water after the rice has been cooked. Rice should therefore, always be cooked in just the amount of water it will absorb. Any water left over should be used for soup or stew, since it will contain valuable B vitamins which should not be wasted.

● Keep cooked rice, if unused, to make salads more substantial.

Brown Rice

Ingredients
300g/11 oz brown rice
1.1 litres/2 pints water
5ml/1 teaspoon salt

Method
1   Bring rice to boil in salted water. Let simmer for 5 minutes without lid then cover and cook on a low heat for about 15 minutes until soft and chewy, but not mushy.
2   To test, stick a knife in the rice and if starting to stick to the bottom of the pan and the knife emerges with cooked grains stuck to it, it's ready!
3   If the rice is almost cooked and there's plenty of liquid in the pan, cook with the lid off until the liquid has evaporated, or drain (saving the liquid!) and cook.
4   If the rice is not cooked but is sticking to the pan bottom, add about 150ml/5 fl oz of water, cover and cook until ready.

Approximate cost of ingredients: 45p

Red Kidney Beans

It is necessary to cook red kidney beans thoroughly or they will cause grave stomach upsets. It is also important to remember not to add any salt to the beans until they are cooked or they may never become tender. For most recipes bring 300g/11 oz beans to the boil in 1.4 litres/2½ pints water. Let boil vigorously for 10 minutes, then cover completely and simmer on a low heat for 2 hours until tender. Test and, if still hard in the centre, cook for a further 30 minutes, adding more water if necessary. I like to cook mine until quite mushy after the starch grain has burst and the water has become sauce-like.

Blackeye Beans

For most recipes bring 300g/11 oz of beans to boil in 1.1 litres/2 pints water. Cover and simmer gently for 30 minutes. Season after the beans have cooked.

Red-Split Lentils

For use in soups 300g/11 oz of lentils will suffice for 1.4 litres/2½ pints of water. Bring to the boil, being careful not to let it boil over as it forms quite a frothy head. Cover and simmer gently for 30 minutes.

For use in flans and loaves measure 250g/9 oz of lentils to 850ml/1½ pints water. Simmer gently without covering, stirring occasionally, for 20–30 minutes until soft and firm. If the lentils are runny cook over a high heat, stirring constantly until firmer. Add a drop more water if the lentils are dry but not cooked and simmer until ready.

Sweet Corn

Corn is another member of the grain family, though it is often served as a vegetable. You can be sure it's high in fibre!

> ● Keep a jar or bottle for all leftover liquids from cooking vegetables or gravy or juices from the cooking of meat. This makes excellent stock for sauces or stews and will keep in the fridge for 2–3 days.

Corn on the Cob

Shuck the corn by removing the leafy wrapping and the thready corn silks. Drop in boiling water and cook for 10–15 minutes. Alternatively, boil in milk and water using ordinary milk or powdered. Serve with butter, salt and pepper, soy sauce etc.

Corn on the cob may also be baked in the oven. Leave the shucks on to retain moisture, and bake for 15–20 minutes in a moderate oven 180°C/350°F (Gas Mark 4). When the outer leaves are beginning to turn brown, it's ready. Peel back the shucks or just pull them off. Pull the silks off the end and serve. This method retains flavour and nutrients lost in boiling.

To remove corn kernels (cooked or raw) from the cob, stand the corn upright in a wide bowl and, holding the upper end, cut downwards along the cob. Delicious in soups, salads and pies etc.

Cornmeal

Besides use in porridge, puddings and cakes, cornmeal is very good in savoury recipes. Use 140g/5 oz of fine cornmeal to 680ml/24 fl oz of milk or water, 10ml/2 teaspoons salt and 30g/1 oz margarine or butter. Bring ingredients to the boil and simmer gently, stirring occasionally.

Corncakes

Ingredients
1 egg
200ml/7 fl oz milk
140g/5 oz fine cornmeal
115g/4 oz canned fish
Salt and freshly ground black pepper

Method
1   Beat the egg and milk and stir in the remaining ingredients.
2   Drop the batter by spoonfuls onto a well-oiled, pre-heated frying pan. Cook over a moderate heat until crisp and golden on both sides, turning only once.
3   Serve hot with salad garnish.

Approximate cost of ingredients: 64p

Popcorn

Method
1   Heat 30ml/2 tablespoons oil in a pan with tight fitting lid.
2   Add 30ml/2 tablespoons popcorn, cover and cook over a moderate heat until corn stops popping.
3   Sprinkle with salt and serve.

Approximate cost of ingredients: 10p

Pastries

Some people are wary about using wholemeal flour in pastries. They find it grainy and heavy, by comparison to the talcum-powder-like flour they've been used to. Often when it comes to rolling it out it breaks and doesn't hold in one piece. Then, to top it all, after baking, it seems so hard and crunchy by comparison to white flour. But it's merely a matter of becoming accustomed to the difference and appreciating the superiority of wholemeal flour!

Once you have kneaded a good dough — not too sticky or not too dry, you should find it comparatively easy to roll out. If the dough crumbles when rolling out — don't panic, knead it again with a drop more water. If the dough is too sticky, add a little more flour. Even if, after rolling out, the dough starts to fragment when rolling it back on the pin ready to place in the flan tin — don't despair, place what remains on the rolling pin in the flan tin and mould on the rest after moistening it a little. After lining the tin with the pastry, if you seem a little short of dough use the trimmings from around the edge of the tin to patch the pastry case. And if you are still a little short — no sweat, the pastry-case will be a little uneven but taste just as nice!

- Keep surplus pastry in a plastic bag in the fridge. It will keep for 2–3 days.

Flan Pastry

Ingredients
115g/4 oz margarine *or* 90ml/3fl oz vegetable oil
225g/½ lb wholemeal flour
A little cold water or milk

Method
1   Rub the margarine into the flour until the mixture resembles fine breadcrumbs. Add a little cold water or milk and knead into a dough.
2   Roll the pastry out evenly on a floured surface. Use to line the flan case (rolling the pastry up onto the rolling pin and unrolling it over the tin).
3   Prick all over the base of the flan with a fork. Partially bake at 170°C/325°F (Gas Mark 3) for 10 minutes.

Approximate cost: 25p

Crumbly Pastry (for pies and pasties)

Ingredients
170g/6 oz margarine
225g/½ lb self-raising wholemeal flour
115g/4 oz plain white flour
A little cold water or milk

Method
1   Rub the fat into the flour until the mixture resembles fine breadcrumbs. Add a little water or milk and knead to a dough.
2   Divide into 2 pieces and roll the larger half for a pie-case and use the remainder for a lid.

Approximate cost: 38p

Dumplings

Ingredients
55g/2 oz margarine
115g/4 oz self-raising wholemeal flour
Salt and freshly ground black pepper
A little water

Method
1   Mix the margarine and the flour, then add just enough
    water to form a stiffish dough.
2   Form into pattie shapes and place on top of soup or
    casserole (arranged around the edge as dumplings in
    the middle take longer to cook) and cook for 10–12
    minutes until swollen. (Alternatively boil in salted water
    10–12 minutes.)
3   Serve immediately as dumplings left immersed too long
    become heavy.

Approximate cost of dumplings: 13p

Chapatis or Quick Bread

Ingredients
170–225g/6–8 oz self-raising wholemeal flour
Salt
A little water
Vegetable oil (6 tablespoons approximately)

Method
1   Form a dough with the water and flour and salt.
2   Form into 6–8 pattie shapes and roll out thinly on a
    floured surface.

3   Fry in a little oil on both sides till golden and crispy. Keep warm in oven until the rest are cooked.
4   Ideal with curries and stew.

Variation:
By adding a few raisins and a little sugar, a quick raisin bread can be made.

Approximate cost of Chapatis or Quick Bread: 19p

Sauces

The basic white sauce in this book is made with wholemeal flour and has a lovely grainy texture which some may find a little unusual. Also, it is made without a roux and is, therefore, less fattening than most other white sauces.

Thin White Sauce

(For cream soups, etc.)

Ingredients
850ml/1½ pints milk
55g/2 oz wholemeal flour

Method
1   Mix 250ml/9 fl oz of milk with the flour into a smooth paste. Stir in a further 250ml/9 fl oz of milk and bring the mixture slowly to the boil over a moderate heat, stirring constantly.
2   Gradually add the rest of the milk, stir and simmer the sauce gently for a further 10 minutes.

Approximate cost of ingredients: 45p

Medium White Sauce

This sauce is used in the Vegetable pies (pages 90 and 91), Fish Pie II (page 100 and 101) and the Savoury Pancake fillings (pages 66,67,68 and 69).

Ingredients
30ml/2 heaped tablespoons wholemeal flour per 285ml/½ pint milk.

Method
1   Gradually mix the flour with the milk into a smooth paste.
2   Bring the mixture to the boil, stirring all the while.
3   Cook for a further 10–15 minutes on a low heat, stirring constantly.

Cheese Sauce

Ingredients
570ml/1 pint medium white sauce
115g/4 oz Cheddar, grated

Method
1   When sauce is made, add cheese and stir until thoroughly blended.

Approximate cost of ingredients: 65p

Parsley Sauce

Ingredients
570ml/1 pint medium white sauce
30ml/2 level tablespoons finely chopped fresh parsley

Method
1　Stir the parsley into the sauce immediately before serving, in order that the parsley may remain very green and retain all its flavour.
2　When serving parsley sauce with fish, 5–10ml/1–2 teaspoons of vinegar may be added to give a piquant flavour.

Approximate cost of ingredients: 36p

Tomato Sauce

Ingredients
2 onions, finely chopped
15ml/1 tablespoon vegetable oil
1 clove garlic, crushed
2.5ml/½ teaspoon mixed herbs
395g/14 oz tin tomatoes
Salt
Freshly ground black pepper

Method
1　Gently sauté the onions in oil with garlic and herbs.
2　Heat the tomatoes in a separate saucepan, crushing them with a wooden spoon.
3　Add the sautéed onion mixture, season, cover and simmer gently 30–45 minutes.
4　Goes well with 'Rice and Mince' (page 114).

Approximate cost of ingredients: 43p

Simple Salad

Although there are a selection of salads available among the recipes for dinners in this book (some of them, a meal in themselves), the Simple Salad is here among the Basic Essentials because it is just that, basically essential to almost all my main meals, eaten with virtually all of them and recommended with nearly every dinner recipe.

Don't buy large amounts of perishables at once. Lettuce will keep well in the fridge for 3 days but watercress should ideally be bought on a daily basis.

Of course, the ingredients listed for a Simple Salad are those I generally use, but should you find yourself short of any of them or with any other vegetables, then vary the combination. The fact is that just about any vegetable eaten cooked can also be eaten raw. So don't let that apple shrivel up, slice it into a salad; don't fry all the onions, chop some into the salad. The only essential ingredient to a Simple Salad is a most elementary oil and vinegar dressing, added five minutes before serving.

If salads aren't already a daily feature of your diet, they should be. You may feel you have to push yourself initially, but it's worth the pushing. Preparation of daily Simple Salad will soon become a 10 minute affair, and much to your benefit!

- In the winter cooked vegetables such as diced potatoes, carrots, beans, cauliflower and beetroot can be used in salad.

Simple Salad

Ingredients
A good helping of lettuce (maybe ½ small round)
½ bunch watercress
1 tomato, sliced
Piece cucumber, sliced
1 carrot, grated

Dressing:
5ml/1 teaspoon salt
Freshly ground black pepper
15ml/1 tablespoon vinegar, to taste
8ml/½ tablespoon oil, to taste

Method
1 Rinse and drain the lettuce and watercress or simply give them a good shake after rinsing. Chop them and place them in the salad bowl then add the other salad ingredients (which should also have been rinsed).
2 Mix the dressing ingredients together and add to the salad just before serving. Toss lightly.

Approximate cost of ingredients: 55p

Yogurt

Basically yogurt is not essential, and when on a budget of £35 per week yogurt is essentially expensive, that is if bought by the carton as most yogurt is. But yogurt is included in the Basic Essentials because it is highly nutritious, low in fat and calories and easy to make. Throughout my time in receipt of Benefit I was also issued with 2 milk tokens per week. These made me eligible for 14 pints of milk, hence if a milk glut was to be avoided and the former luxury yogurt enjoyed, making my own was the solution. Furthermore, yogurt is very adaptable and can be used in both sweet and savoury dishes, is an excellent and convenient starter for babies and is easy to digest. Indeed, any member of a household can benefit greatly by consuming more yogurt.

Unfortunately, store-bought varieties can prove to be expensive, and the highly flavoured pots available can be quite adulterated with additives. I find it simple and economical to make my own. You don't have to own a farm house to make yogurt, it's really quite convenient once you know how and positively indulgent creating your own wholesome flavours. Those over-ripe strawberries you bought cheaply make an excellent addition: yogurt drinks are delicious and can be thinned down with water or fruit juice and yogurt dressings and dips are very appetizing. In fact, yogurt is extremely versatile.

It is not necessary to have a yogurt maker, but some find that using one makes the process easier. I use just an ordinary enamelled, cast-iron casserole with a lid, and it does the job well enough for me. A heavy glass casserole or earthenware pot with lid can be used equally successfully and incubated in a *warm* (not hot) oven, a warm airing cupboard or simply near a hot radiator. Alternatively, a thermos flask can be used.

● To scald food or milk: pour boiling water over food and let stand for a few minutes. To scald milk is to bring it almost to the boil.

Non-fat Dry-milk Yogurt

Ingredients
(Makes 850ml/1½ pints of yogurt)

115g/4 oz non-fat dry-milk powder (or more if a richer
   concentration is desired)
720ml/1¼ pints hot water
60ml/2 fl oz plain yogurt (commercial or home-made)

Method
1   Beat or blend milk powder with hot water until all the
    granules are dissolved (an electric blender is fine at this
    stage). Then pour the mixture into the container and beat
    the yogurt in lightly (being careful to ensure that the
    mixture is not too hot and is around 55°C/110°F).
2   Cover and incubate. It is important to *remember not to
    move* the container during this period or the yogurt will
    separate. The yogurt should set within 3½ hours. If after
    that time it hasn't, repeat the process and use a fresh
    commercial starter.

Fresh Milk Yogurt

All milk must first be scalded (brought almost to the boil) to kill off any bacteria that might prevent the growth of yogurt culture. The milk must next be left to cool down until it is hand-hot (55°C/110°F).

Ingredients
1.1 litres/2 pints milk (skimmed or whole)
55g/2 oz dry milk powder
60ml/2 fl oz unflavoured yogurt (commercial or home-made)

Method
1   Scald the milk then add the milk powder whilst the milk is still very hot. If desired, the mixture can be made smoother by pouring through a fine strainer and forcing through with a small wooden spoon.
2   Leave to cool for approximately 15 minutes then add a little milk to the yogurt and beat lightly with a fork.
3   Add this to the rest of the milk and beat briefly. Incubate as outlined above. (Makes 1.1 litres/2 pints.)

Frying Pan with Lid

The reason for inclusion of this one most inedible item among the Basic Essentials is that the method of cooking most frequently employed when preparing the many dishes in this book is to sauté (fry lightly in a little oil). Covering the frying pan with a lid will help retain both heat and moisture, reduce frying time, make the kitchen less hot and steamy and ensure the foods cooked retain maximum flavour.

Sadly, good cast-iron frying pans with lids can prove difficult to find and as my own orange enamelled pan-set did not include one, I improvised and successfully used the slightly narrower lid of the casserole dish, in a slightly sunken position to cover all my fast-frying-meals.

Care of your cast-iron pan

It is important after using a frying pan for meat and certain other dishes, apart from merely sautéing vegetables, to wash and rinse it out thoroughly. After that it helps to wipe it with a clean cloth then dry it over a low heat. Add 15ml/1 tablespoon of oil and tilt pan so that the oil spreads around. This prevents the pan from rusting.

Hints — Tips — and Suggestions

On buying vegetables

When buying vegetables see that the green ones are not yellow but a fresh green colour and crisp. Root vegetables should be firm and not coarse. Tomatoes should be firm and red but if bought a little green can be ripened in a dark drawer. Potatoes should be firm and have no shoots. Lettuce and other salad vegetables should be crisp.

On boiling vegetables

Most vegetables should be cooked in a small amount of water and covered while cooking. When cooking frozen peas add 15ml/1 tablespoon water, 1 knob of margarine or butter and a little salt. Double the amount of water when cooking fresh peas. Cover the peas (455g/1 lb frozen) and cook on a very low light, stirring occasionally, for about 10–15 minutes. Greens can be shredded and cooked by the 455g/1 lb with 60ml/4 tablespoons water, a knob of margarine or butter and salt. Cook until tender but not soggy. Spinach should not be shredded but covered and cooked with a drop of water and a knob of margarine and seasoned to taste. Cook on a low heat for about 5 minutes. Once the vegetables are cooked, strain them and save the liquid for stocks and soups.

2
Breakfasts

Breakfast time in most households tends to be a rather rushed part of the day. Even in a home where the bread-winner has been effectively grounded with no workplace to get to, if there are youngsters either hurrying out to, or to be taken out to school, then the pressure (to get them washed, dressed, fed and out) remains on at breakfast time.

This, the rushed nature of breakfast time, must be a major factor in the monumental success over the years of the numerous so-called 'breakfast cereals' available on the shelves of every supermarket. Preparation of these 'break-fasts' is merely a matter of pouring them into a bowl, covering them with milk and (if not already caked in sugar coating) showering them with sugar (though I did once know a boy who put sugar even on sugared cereal), to be then gobbled down most enthusiastically in minutes by non-complaining youngsters.

Many such products boast graphs or lists of their mineral or vitamin content, placed strategically upon the sides of their boxes to dazzle and impress their consumer whilst wolfing them down at the table. But all too often these are artificially produced vitamins added to an otherwise relat-ively deficient product and, even in the cases of the few such breakfast cereals where the product is quite fibrous and without additives, one pays dearly for the little one gets. (I do recall reading many years ago in a national daily of an outbreak of mice in a factory producing a leading breakfast cereal. The result of this was extensive rodential damage to the outer cardboard boxes, the costly contents of which went untouched. Anything mice have the sense to leave alone can't be too nourishing!)

I myself have long regarded all boxed cereals containing artificial flavouring, colouring or preservatives, as many do, most unsuitable for a good breakfast and, luckily, I never did start any of my kids on breakfast cereals. Artificial colouring is (in my books) particularly important to avoid because it is being increasingly recognized as a factor in hyperactivity among sensitive children and is also an often unsuspected cause of much discomfort and suffering when it triggers allergies of which many of us are wholly unaware.

Finally, all such cereals rely heavily upon the milk in which they are soaked to nourish their consumer as they lack any of their own natural staying power, hence we have seen the advent of elevenses — when many of those reliant upon such breakfasts are seen ravenously eating snacks of sorts — usually further produce of the junk food giants.

Thus the truth of the matter is that should you or members of your household have been reliant upon such products for some time, then both you and the kids would be better off, in terms of nourishment as well as cash in the pocket, simply by serving yourselves a bowl of oats with a few raisins added (Miser's Muesli) or sitting down to a bowl of hot and hearty porridge for your breakfasts.

Of course, initially, least enthusiastic to give up their morning meals of mass produced breakfast cereals may be the children. But when it comes to the crunch I do urge you to persevere because kids, not so set in their ways, are quite flexible and can quickly adapt themselves to changes, unlike most of us adults, and if your kids understand that their newly adopted set of meals is not only going to be better for them in terms of health, but is also going to enable you to give them more pocket money or funding for that long sought garment or special activity, their co-operation should be achieved without too much difficulty.

So here are some 13 suggestions for breakfasts. All are

- Separate the weekly shopping budget from all your other money: this way you can see visibly when you are invading your other monies.

---

eaten in this household, though some are naturally more occasional than others: Simple Bread Cereal, for instance, is usually a last resort. Several of these preparations were a craze for some time — that is literally the only breakfast eaten day after day, for weeks on end. But the one single food eaten most frequently by ourselves for breakfast over the years must be toast — good old wholemeal toast, that is. When it comes to spreads, or toppings, each member of our household seems to have a particular preference: maybe peanut butter or yeast extract or marmalade, but nobody ever seems to tire of good old wholemeal toast, day in day out, year after year, toast is a favourite for their breakfast.

Oat Porridge

(Serves 4–6)

Ingredients
115g/4 oz porridge oats
850ml–1.1 litres/1½–2 pints milk (whole, skimmed or re-constituted)

Method
1   Bring oats and milk to the boil, stirring occasionally. Simmer 2–5 minutes, stirring all the time.
2   Serve with brown sugar or honey. Nut, seed or soy milks may also be used.

Approximate cost: 50p

Miser's Muesli

(1 serving)

Ingredients
55g/2 oz porridge oats
15–30ml/1–2 tablespoons seedless raisins or sultanas
150ml/5 fl oz milk (whole, skimmed or soy etc.)

Method
1   Mix oatmeal with the dried fruit. Sprinkle with brown sugar or honey if desired. (To reduce the amount of sweetening needed, add 2.5ml/$\frac{1}{2}$ teaspoon vanilla extract to each 240ml/8 fl oz of milk.)
2   Top with milk or yogurt sweetened with honey (30ml/2 tablespoons yogurt — 5ml/1 teaspoon honey).
3   Can also be served with sliced banana, peaches or any berry in season.

Approximate cost: 20p

Cornmeal Porridge

(6–8 servings)

Ingredients
140g/5 oz cornmeal (fine)
1.1–1.7 litres/2–2$\frac{1}{2}$ pints milk (whole, re-constituted or soy etc.)

Method
1   Stir cornmeal with the milk. Bring to the boil, cook 10 minutes stirring often.
2   Sweeten with brown sugar or honey. Serve hot.

Approximate cost: 73p

Cornmeal Pudding

(6–8 servings)

Ingredients
140g/5 oz cornmeal (fine)
850ml–1.1 litres/1½–2 pints milk

Method
1   Stir the cornmeal into the milk. Bring to the boil and cook
    for 10 minutes, stirring often.
2   Serve the hot thick cornmeal with butter or cottage
    cheese and salt or jam.

Approximate cost: 52p

Toast Cereal

(Serves 6)

Ingredients
6 slices wholemeal bread
15ml/1 tablespoon honey or brown sugar
450ml/¾ pint milk

Method
1   Toast, lightly butter and dice the bread. Divide into
    serving bowls.
2   Sweeten the milk with honey or sugar. Heat, then pour
    over the toast cubes.

Approximate cost: 48p

Bread Cereal

(Serves 6)

Ingredients
6 slices wholemeal bread
90ml/6 tablespoons seedless raisins or sultanas
450ml/¾ pint milk

Method
1   Dice and divide bread into serving bowls.
2   Sprinkle with raisins and, if desired, brown sugar.
3   Heat milk and pour onto bread cubes.

Approximate cost: 68p

Grilled Banana

(1 serving)

Ingredients
1 medium banana

Method
1   Make a slit in banana skin from end to end. Grill under a
    moderate heat for 10 minutes.
2   Serve in peel with jam and yogurt inserted in the slit.

Approximate cost: 18p

Popcorn Surprise

(Serves 6–8)

Ingredients
45ml/3 tablespoons vegetable oil
45ml/3 tablespoons popcorn
450–570ml/¾–1 pint milk

Method
1   Heat the oil in a pan with a tight fitting lid (a large pan or pressure cooker is ideal for this). Add popcorn and cover. The corn will start to pop as it cooks over a moderate heat.
2   When the popping sounds cease the popcorn is ready.
3   Sweeten to taste with brown sugar and add milk.

Approximate cost: 50p

Honey – Corn Puffs

(Serves 6–8)

Ingredients
2 oz margarine
3 tablespoons popcorn
1 tablespoon honey
1 pint milk

Method
1   Melt the margarine in a large lidded pan. Add popcorn and cover. The popcorn will start to pop as it cooks over a moderately high heat.
2   When the popping sounds cease the popcorn is ready.
3   Whilst warm stir in the honey. Serve with milk.

Approximate cost: 68p

Eggs — Basic Methods of Cooking

Softboiled
Lower gently into boiling water and simmer gently for 3 minutes. If put into cold water, bring gently to the boil and simmer gently for $2\frac{1}{2}$–3 minutes. After the eggs have cooked plunge them into cold water to prevent them cooking further with their own heat. Eggs taken from the refrigerator often require an extra $\frac{1}{2}$–1 minute cooking and the cold water method is best. 5ml/1 level teaspoon of salt in the cooking water will help to prevent the shells cracking. If the shells crack, 5ml/1 teaspoon of vinegar will help to prevent the egg white from dispersing in the water.

Hard-boiled
Gently simmer eggs for 15 minutes. Eggs lowered into boiling water are more likely to have their yolks in the centre than those put into cold water. To avoid a dark ring around the yolk, do not over-boil, and do plunge the eggs after cooking into cold water.

Coddled
Place eggs in their shells in a pan of boiling water. Cover and remove pan from heat. Leave for 10 minutes, then serve.

Poached
Have ready a shallow pan containing lightly-salted water. Break eggs, one at a time, into a cup or saucer and slip gently into the simmering water. Cover and remove pan from heat, and leave in a warm place until whites have set and a thin film has formed over the yolks. Lift them out with a perforated spoon, and serve on buttered toast. If an egg poacher is used, butter shells before breaking an egg into each. Cover and steam until set.

Scrambled Eggs

Ingredients
4 eggs
Salt and freshly ground black pepper
30ml/2 tablespoons milk
30g/1 oz margarine or butter

Method
1   Beat the eggs with seasoning and milk.
2   Melt the margarine or butter in a small saucepan, pour in the egg mixture and stir over a moderate heat until the mixture has set creamily but is still moist.
3   Alternatively, melt the fat (or use vegetable oil) then beat the eggs, seasoning and milk in the pan with a wooden spoon. Cook as before.

Approximate cost of ingredients: 40p

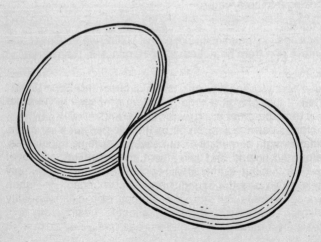

3
Lunches

Almost all the recipes for lunches in this book are substantial enough to serve as a main meal or as the main part of a dinner. All, that is, with the exception of sweet pancakes, perhaps. Thus, it is no strange thing in this household to sit down at dinner-time to Cream of Mackerel Soup served with a heap of bread buns and garnished with watercress, or Savoury Pancakes with baked potatoes and salad.

But, after having baked bread earlier in the morning but not having yet gone out to the shops, it is often very convenient to use up the few vegetables remaining in the cupboard or remnants (of either fish or meat) from last night's dinner in a soup, most convenient. Hence, it is usually in the last hour of the morning that I find myself preparing soups, soups to be consumed for lunch. Likewise, the ingredients for a Savoury Pancake filling such as Sweet Corn and Mushrooms or Cream Cheese and Spinach will often be available to use up, and when wrapped in a pancake they become great favourites with the kids.

Now, upon reading some of the recipes for soups, the initial thought of making a sauce while sautéing vegetables, before mixing and seasoning them, may seem rather a lot of needless labour to many non-cooks when one can simply open a tin, warm the contents and — abracadabra — lunch (a soup) is ready. But there is no comparison in either quality or cost. You're best off in both respects making your own meals, real meals. In my earliest days rendered jobless, it was the newly discovered activity of preparing quality meals which proved a great alternative to those idle hours of twiddling thumbs, which is when the erosion of one's morale can otherwise set in.

However, having said all that, I must confess that in my opinion nothing beats bread as a base for lunches. I never tire of it, nor will you if you're making the real stuff! The choice is endless, toasted or not, anything from smoked salmon sandwiches to banana butties, pâtés, cooked meats, cheeses and vegetables spreads. For quickness, ease and convenience, in my opinion, at lunch-time, 'nowt beats butties!'

Welsh Rarebit

(Serves 2–3)

Ingredients
115g/4 oz grated cheese
45ml/3 tablespoon milk
Salt and freshly ground black pepper
15ml/1 tablespoon margarine or butter
4–6 slices toast

Method
1   Place the cheese and milk in a saucepan and melt slowly.
2   Add the pepper, salt and margarine or butter.
3   When hot, pour over the toast and brown under the grill until bubbling. (Sometimes a little beer is added to the mixture.)

Approximate cost of ingredients: 53p

Sardines on Toast

Ingredients
120g/4¼ oz tin sardines
55g/2 oz grated cheese
15ml/1 tablespoon margarine or butter
Salt and freshly ground black pepper
15ml/1 tablespoon milk or yogurt
4–6 slices toast

Method
1   Mash the sardines and combine with most of the cheese and the other ingredients.
2   Pile the mixture on the toast. Sprinkle with the remaining cheese and brown under the grill.

Approximate cost of ingredients: 65p

Sandwich suggestions (priced and unpriced)

Taramasalata and salad on wholemeal bread (12 slices) 85p.
Humous spread and salad on wholemeal bread (12 slices) 79p.
Mackerel pâté and salad on wholemeal bread (12 slices) 95p.
Ham and salad on wholemeal bread (12 slices) £1.45.
Crab pâté and salad on wholemeal bread (12 slices) £1.10.
Chicken and salad on wholemeal bread.
Tuna fish and sweetcorn on wholemeal bread.
Smoked mackerel mashed with yogurt garnished with thinly sliced orange.
Tinned sardines (pilchards) mashed with yogurt or salad cream and black pepper.

Cottage cheese and olives on wholemeal bread.

Cold cooked beans mashed with yeast extract, herbs and garnished with salad.

Yeast extract, cheese and salad on wholemeal bread.

Hard-boiled eggs and grated cheese mashed with salad cream or yogurt with black pepper.

Hard-boiled eggs and salad with salad cream or yogurt dressing.

Scrambled egg on its own or with sweetcorn or mushroom.

Toasted cheese sandwich (12 slices) with salad £1.00.

Baked beans on toast (8 slices) 80p.

- Cutting fresh new bread can prove difficult if still warm. Hence, if unable to wait for bread to cool stand the knife in boiling water for a few minutes first.

Omelettes – Basic Method

If possible keep a special pan for omelette making, and wipe out with paper after use to preserve an oily surface. For a 3–4 egg omelette you will need a pan about 23cm/9 inches in diameter, and for a 6 egg omelette, the pan should be about 25cm/10 inches in diameter.

Eggs for omelettes should not be beaten too much: 30 seconds' beating with a fork is sufficient. Do not let the butter in the pan brown or the omelette may stick. Never mix milk with eggs for omelettes as it will make them tough.

Chinese Omelette

Ingredients
4 eggs
60ml/4 tablespoon water
Salt and freshly ground black pepper
4 onions, finely chopped
55g/2 oz beansprouts
30ml/2 tablespoons vegetable oil
225g/½ lb cooked lean pork or chicken, diced

Method
1   Lightly beat the eggs. Add water and seasoning and whisk together.
2   In a pan other than the one to be used for the omelette, sauté the onion and beansprouts in a little oil. Add the cooked meat and continue to stir-fry until the onion is tender and the mixture piping hot.
3   Heat the omelette pan, add a little oil and when hot, add half the egg mixture. When the bottom of the egg mixture has set, spoon over a layer of meat mixture.
4   Cover with more of the egg and continue to cook like an omelette, shaking the pan occasionally until the mixture has almost set. Turn over and brown the other side.
5   Suitable for lunch or for dinner with hot rice and soya sauce.

Approximate cost of ingredients: £1.40

Yorkshire Omelette

Ingredients
4 potatoes, cooked
115g/4 oz bacon
30ml/2 tablespoon vegetable oil
5 eggs
2.5ml/$\frac{1}{2}$ teaspoon mixed herbs
Salt and freshly ground black pepper

Method
1   Cut the potatoes and bacon into small pieces and fry the bacon first and then the potatoes, in the vegetable oil.
2   Beat the eggs, add the bacon, potatoes, herbs and seasoning.
3   Cook until the mixture has almost set then turn and brown the other side. Serve flat.

Approximate cost of ingredients: 90p

Cheese Omelette

Ingredients
6 eggs
15ml/1 tablespoon cold water
Salt and freshly ground black pepper
30g/1 oz butter or margarine
55g/2 oz grated cheese

Method
1   Beat the eggs and water with a fork for 30 seconds. Add seasoning.
2   Melt the butter in an omelette pan and when it is sizzling hot but not brown, add the eggs.

3 · Sprinkle over the cheese and cook over a moderate
   heat, lifting the edges so that the uncooked part can run
   underneath. When it is firm but still soft on top it is ready.
4 Fold the omelette over the cheese and serve either with
   wholemeal bread at lunchtime or with baked potatoes
   and salad at dinner time.

Approximate cost of ingredients: 74p

Ham Omelette

Ingredients
1 onion, chopped
15ml/1 tablespoon vegetable oil
115g/4 oz cooked ham, diced
6 eggs

Method
1 Sauté the onion until soft, add the ham and continue
   cooking for 1–2 minutes. Pour on the beaten eggs.
2 Stir once or twice with a fork and lift the edges so that the
   uncooked part can run underneath.
3 When set, fold over and serve either at lunch or dinner
   time.

Approximate cost of ingredients: £1.17

Mushroom Omelette

Ingredients
115g/4 oz mushrooms, chopped
15ml/1 tablespoon vegetable oil
5ml/ 1 teaspoon lemon juice
Salt and freshly ground black pepper
6 eggs

Method
1   Sauté the mushrooms in the oil, lemon juice and seasoning for 30 seconds then cover and cook over a gentle
heat for 5 minutes.
2   Meanwhile, beat the eggs with 15ml/1 tablespoon of
water and seasoning and use this mixture to make an
omelette.
3   When it has set, fill with the mushrooms mixture, fold
over and serve immediately.

Approximate cost of ingredients: 85p

Pancakes
Savoury Pancakes

(Makes 8–10)

Ingredients
225g/$\frac{1}{2}$ lb wholemeal flour
Pinch salt
2 eggs
1 pint milk

Method
1   Mix the flour and salt. Make a well in the centre and
break in the eggs. Add the milk gradually and beat well to

make a smooth batter. Or mix the batter in a blender, starting with the milk and eggs and gradually adding the flour.

2   Heat 1–2 teaspoons oil in a frying pan (preferably cast iron). Tilt the pan so that the oil spreads evenly all over. When the pan is hot pour in up to 2 tablespoons batter and tilt the pan so that the batter spreads evenly. Cook over a moderate heat until bubbles form on the surface. Slide a spatula under the pancake and flip it over to cook the other side.

3   Ideally the pancake should be filled and served immediately. If not, keep pancakes in a warm oven on a plate covered with another plate until ready to fill.

Approximate cost of ingredients: 67p

Chicken or Fish and Mushroom Filling

Ingredients
$\frac{1}{4}$ cooked chicken or 455g/1 lb fish fillets
285ml/$\frac{1}{2}$ pint medium white sauce
55g/2 oz mushrooms, sautéed
Salt and freshly ground black pepper

Method
1   Shred the chicken or flake the cooked fish and mix with the sauce. Add the cooked mushrooms and season to taste.
2   Fill each pancake with 15ml/1 tablespoon of the mixture and roll each one up.
3   Lay them side by side in a greased baking dish and cook in a moderate oven at 180°C/350°F (Gas Mark 4) for about 15 minutes.

Approximate cost of ingredients: £1.90

Mushroom, Onion and Beansprout Pancake Filling

Ingredients
55g/2 oz mushrooms, sliced
1 onion, sliced
115g/4 oz beansprouts, chopped
15–30ml/1–2 tablespoons vegetable oil
15ml/1 tablespoon soya sauce

Method
1   Sauté the vegetables in a little oil for 10 minutes.
2   Add the soya sauce and use to fill pancakes.

Approximate cost of ingredients for 4 savoury pancakes: £1.10p

Sweetcorn and Mushroom Pancake Filling

Ingredients
1 onion, sliced
55g/2 oz mushrooms, sliced
115g/4 oz fresh sweetcorn kernels (or frozen)
15–30ml/1–2 tablespoons vegetable oil
285ml/½ pint medium white sauce

Method
1 Sauté the vegetables in a little oil for 10–15 minutes.
2 Add the white sauce, season and use to fill pancakes.

Approximate cost of ingredients for 4 savoury
pancakes: £1.20

Cream Cheese and Spinach Pancake Filling

Ingredients
1 onion, sliced
15ml/1 tablespoon vegetable oil
225g/$\frac{1}{2}$ lb spinach, washed and chopped
115g/4 oz cream cheese

Method
1 Sauté the onion in oil for 5 minutes. Add the spinach and
   sauté for a further 5–10 minutes.
2 Take off the heat and stir in the cream cheese. Use to fill
   the pancakes.

Approximate cost of ingredients for 4 savoury
pancakes: £1.44

Pancakes (Sweet)

Ingredients
3 eggs
285ml/½ pint milk
115g/4 oz wholemeal flour
Vegetable oil
Honey and lemon
Fruit of choice

Method
1   Add the eggs and milk gradually to the flour and beat well to make a smooth batter. Alternatively, mix the batter in a blender starting with the eggs and milk and gradually adding the flour.
2   Heat approximately 2 teaspoons oil in a frying pan (preferably cast-iron) and tilt the pan so that the oil spreads evenly.
3   When the pan is hot pour in up to 2 tablespoons batter and tilt the pan so that the batter spreads evenly.
4   Cook over a moderate heat until bubbles form on the surface. Slide a spatula under the pancake and flip it over to cook the other side.
5   Ideally fill and serve immediately or keep pancakes in a warm oven on a plate covered with another plate until ready to fill.
6   To serve, spread each pancake with honey and lemon and fill with sliced bananas, peaches or strawberries or ice cream, or a mixture. Or, if preferred, serve with Greek yogurt.

Approximate cost of ingredients for 6–8 pancakes: 94p

Soups

Tomato Bouillon

Ingredients
300g/11 oz jar tomato purée
850ml/1½ pints stock (or water with 15ml/1 tablespoon yeast
   extract)
5ml/1 teaspoon brown sugar
Salt and freshly ground black pepper
Finely chopped parsley

Method
1   Bring the tomato purée and stock to the boil. Add the
    sugar and seasoning to taste.
2   Sprinkle with chopped parsley and serve with toast.

Approximate cost of ingredients: 70p

Mulligatawny Soup

Ingredients
300g/11 oz split red lentils
850ml–1 litre/1½–2 pints stock (or water with 15ml/1 table-
    spoon yeast extract)
15ml/1 tablespoon curry powder
15ml/1 tablespoon vegetable oil
2 carrots, grated
2 onions, sliced
1 apple, cored and chopped
Crushed garlic to taste
Salt
Juice ½ lemon

Method
1   Bring the lentils to the boil in the stock with the curry
    powder.
2   Meanwhile, heat the oil and sauté the carrots, onions,
    apple and garlic for 15 minutes.
3   Add the vegetables to the stock and simmer for 30
    minutes. Season and stir in lemon juice.

Approximate cost of ingredients: £1.11

Minestrone Soup

Ingredients
55g/2 oz wholewheat spaghetti, broken into small pieces
850ml–1 litre/1½–2 pints stock (or water with 15ml/
    1 tablespoon yeast extract)
55g/2 oz chopped bacon, optional
115g/4 oz porridge oats
115g/4 oz cabbage, finely chopped
1 turnip, grated
1 onion, sliced
Oil, as necessary
Salt and freshly ground black pepper
Pinch dried or freshly chopped thyme

Method
1   Bring the spaghetti to the boil in the stock.
2   Sauté the bacon, oats and vegetables with a little oil if
    necessary, for 15 minutes. Add them to the soup stock
    and simmer for 30 minutes. Season to taste.

Approximate cost of ingredients: 70p

• A ham bone, or bits of left-over ham and bacon make a good stock and go especially well with lentils.

Lentil Soup

Ingredients
300g/11 oz red split lentils
1.1 litres/2 pints water
3 carrots, grated
2 onions, sliced
Crushed garlic, to taste
1 medium leek, chopped
15ml/1 tablespoon vegetable oil (soya etc.)
15ml/ 1 tablespoon soya sauce
7.5ml/½ tablespoon tomato purée
Salt and freshly ground black pepper

Method
1 Bring the lentils to the boil in the water.
2 Sauté the vegetables in oil for 15 minutes and add to soup stock. Add the soya sauce and tomato purée. Season and simmer for 25 minutes.
3 Serve with wholemeal bread or dumplings.

Approximate cost of Lentil Soup: £1.08

Cream of Mackerel Soup

Ingredients
1 carrot, grated
Onion, sliced
Crushed garlic, to taste
15ml/1 tablespoon vegetable oil
1 small mackerel, filleted
55g/2 oz mushrooms, sliced
30ml/2 tablespoons finely chopped parsley
55g/2 oz wholemeal flour
850ml–l litre/1½–2 pints milk (or milk and water)
Salt and freshly ground black pepper

Method
1   Sauté the carrot, onion and garlic in oil for 10 minutes. Add the fish, cover and cook for a further 10 minutes. Add the mushrooms and parsley.
2   Meanwhile, make a white sauce using the Basic White Sauce method (page 42). Simmer the sauce gently for 5–10 minutes stirring often and thin down if liked with more milk or water (about 285ml/½ pint).
3   Add the cooked vegetables and fish, stir well and season. The fish should flake nicely and the soup turn golden.

Approximate cost of ingredients: £1.44

Cream of Chicken Soup

Ingredients
1 small piece chicken
15ml/1 tablespoon vegetable oil
2 stalks celery, chopped
1 onion, sliced
55g/2 oz frozen peas
55g/2 oz wholemeal flour
850ml-l litre/1½-2 pints milk (or milk and water)
Salt and freshly ground black pepper

Method
1   If not using cooked chicken, sauté the chicken in the oil
    for 15 minutes in a covered pan then add the vegetables,
    stir, cover and sauté for a further 10–15 minutes.
2   Meanwhile, make a white sauce using the Basic White
    Sauce method (page 42).
3   Bone and shred the chicken and add it to the white sauce
    with the vegetables. Stir, season and serve with bread
    dough dumplings or bargain bread.

Approximate cost of ingredients: £1.78

Variation:

Boxing Day Soup

Follow the Cream of Chicken Soup recipe substituting turkey
for the chicken.

Cream of Mushroom Soup

Ingredients
1 carrot, grated
1 onion, sliced
115g/4 oz mushrooms, chopped
15ml/1 tablespoon vegetable oil
55g/2 oz wholemeal flour
850ml–l litre/1½–2 pints milk
Salt and freshly ground black pepper

Method
1   Sauté the carrot, onion and mushrooms in the vegetable oil for about 15 minutes.
2   Meanwhile make a white sauce from the flour and milk using the Basic White Sauce method (page 42).
3   Add the vegetables, season and cook for a further 10–15 minutes, stirring occasionally.
4   Serve with wholemeal bread or dumplings.

Approximate cost of ingredients: 94p

Cream of Celery Soup

Ingredients
6 celery stalks, diced
1 onion, sliced
1 small bunch parsley, finely chopped
15ml/1 tablespoon vegetable oil
55g/2 oz wholemeal flour
850ml–l litre/1½–2 pints milk (or milk and water)
Salt and freshly ground black pepper

Method
1   Sauté the celery, onion and parsley in vegetable oil for 15 minutes.
2   Make a white sauce with the flour and milk using the Basic White Sauce method (page 42).
3   Add the vegetables, season and cook for a further 10–15 minutes. Serve with wholemeal bread or dumplings.

Approximate cost of ingredients: 94p

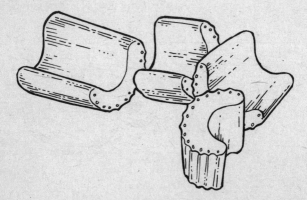

Spring Vegetable Soup

Ingredients
115g/4 oz fresh or frozen peas
1 stick celery, chopped
1 young carrot, grated
1 medium onion, sliced
55g/2 oz mushrooms, chopped
15ml/1 tablespoon vegetable oil
55g/2 oz wholemeal flour
850ml–l litre/1½–2 pints milk (or milk and water)
Salt and freshly ground black pepper

Method
1   Sauté the vegetables in the oil for 15 minutes.
2   Make a white sauce with the flour and milk using the
    Basic White Sauce method (page 42).
3   Add the vegetables and seasoning to the sauce. Cook for
    a further 10–15 minutes, stirring occasionally.

Approximate cost of ingredients: 90p

4
Main Meals

Now last, but by no means least, are the dinner recipes, not all dinners in themselves but it's at dinner time that I tend to serve them. Two of these meals are weekly preparations in this kitchen: Roast Chicken and Quick Quiche. Week in, week out, nobody tires of them and there'd be some jolly stern questions from the kids to answer should I let a week pass without them. But for the remaining five nights of the week I refer to my dinner list, in order to keep our menu varied but within budget, and suggest that you do likewise.

It often helps to plan a meal in advance, for example, when making Cowboy Beans, if wishing to have dinner at 5 o'clock, it's best to put the beans on to cook at 2 o'clock. Alternatively, red kidney beans can be cooked in large batches and some frozen for future use. Those persons cooking for themselves or two people at the most can freeze the surplus or divide the ingredients in the recipes more or less in half.

If some of the recipes don't turn out quite right — don't despair, try again! Don't lose confidence, you'll soon get the hang of it. Your creation may not look nice, but if you've basically stuck by the recipe, it will be very edible! (So many of our meals today are designed to please the eye but not the belly.) Cooking is a science, a domestic science, and you mustn't be afraid to experiment — if you feel like substituting the vegetables in a recipe for some others, do so. Go ahead, have fun and, above all, relax!

On pages 137–140 there are some exemplary menus. Each is for an entire week's meals and each week's selection should be attainable within the figure of £35. use these as an initial guide and you should soon be selecting your own combinations to suit both your taste and your pocket.

- When freezing make up large batches of burgers, rissoles, fishcakes, stews, soups, main meals, etc. Food will also keep for several days in a fridge.

Blackeye Beanburgers

(Serves 4)

Ingredients
300g/11 oz blackeye beans
1.1 litres/2 pints water
Salt and freshly ground black pepper
2 small onions, chopped
3 cloves garlic, crushed
60ml/4 tablespoons vegetable oil
170g/6 oz sage and onion stuffing
Flour, for shaping
1 beaten egg for binding (optional)

Method
1   Boil the beans in the water for 10 minutes. Lower the heat, cover and simmer for 1 hour (do not add salt until cooked). When cooked, season the beans.
2   Sauté the onions and garlic in 15ml/1 tablespoon of the oil and add them with the stuffing to the lentils. Mash with a potato masher. If using egg, allow to cool before adding to mixture. Then shape into burgers and roll them in a little flour.
3   Leave to stand on a wire rack for 10 minutes then fry in oil for about 10 minutes on each side or bake in oil at 200°C/400°F (Gas Mark 6) for 10 minutes, adding more oil if necessary. Serve with baked potatoes and salad.

Approximate cost of ingredients: £1.08

● Try to maximize oven use e.g., cook burgers in a roasting tin and, instead of boiling potatoes, bake potatoes on the top rung of the oven at the same time.

Variation:

Redbean Burgers

(Serves 4)

Method
Substitute 300g/11 oz of red kidney beans for the blackeye beans in the recipe above simmering the red beans for 2 hours (or if they have been soaked overnight, simmer for $1\frac{1}{2}$ hours, or pressure cook for 15 minutes). Continue as for blackeye burgers using the same ingredients.

Approximate cost of ingredients: £1.15

Blackeye Bean Stew with Dumplings

Ingredients
455g/1 lb potatoes chopped
150g/5½ oz blackeye beans
1.7 litres/3 pints water
10ml/2 teaspoons yeast extract
2 carrots, sliced
4 onions, sliced
Crushed garlic, to taste
Piece cucumber, chopped large
8ml/½ tablespoon tomato purée
Salt and freshly ground black pepper

Dumplings:
115g/4 oz wholemeal flour (1 cup)
55g/2 oz margarine
Salt and freshly ground black pepper
A little water

Method
1 Bring the potatoes and beans to the boil with the yeast extract. Cover and simmer.
2 Sauté the vegetables, starting with the carrots and ending with the cucumber, for 10–15 minutes. Combine the vegetables with the beans and potatoes.
3 Add the tomato purée and season with salt and pepper. Cover and simmer gently for 10–15 minutes.
4 Add the dumplings (see page 40 of Basic Essentials), cover and cook for a further 10 minutes till the dumplings swell. Serve immediately.

Alternatively:
Replace the blackeye beans with 300g/11 oz red split lentils. This can be cooked in the oven as a casserole. Prepare the

beans and vegetables as before. Place in a casserole and bake at a moderate heat for 15–20 minutes. Add the dumplings during the last 10 minutes.

Approximate cost of ingredients: 98p

Quick Quiche

(Serves 4)

Ingredients
225g/½ lb wholemeal flour
115g/4 oz margarine
A little cold water, to mix
3 medium onions, chopped
30–45ml/2–3 tablespoons vegetable oil
225g/½ lb grated Cheddar
3 eggs
Salt and freshly ground black pepper

Method
1 Rub the flour and margarine together to make a bread-crumb-like mixture. Add a little cold water to form a dough and use to line a flan case. Prick all over with a fork and bake blind at 170°C/325°F (Gas Mark 3) for 10 minutes.
2 Sauté the onion in a little oil over a low heat for 5–10 minutes. Take off the heat and add the cheese beaten with the eggs. Season and turn into the pastry case.
3 Bake at 200°C/400°F (Gas Mark 6) on the second shelf from the top for 15–20 minutes or until the filling is golden. Serve with baked potatoes and salad.

Approximate cost of ingredients: £1.35

● To bake blind means to bake a pastry case without a filling. To prevent shrinkage stab with a fork.

Vegetable Curry

Ingredients

2 carrots, grated
1 stick celery, chopped
1 green pepper, sliced
Crushed garlic, to taste
4 small onions, sliced
30–45ml/2–3 tablespoons vegetable oil
55g/2 oz mushrooms, sliced
3 cooked potatoes
15ml/1 tablespoon raisins
395g/14 oz tin tomatoes
25ml/5 teaspoons curry powder
Salt
30ml/2 tablespoons soya sauce
15ml/1 tablespoon tomato purée

Method

1 Sauté the vegetables in the oil beginning with the carrots, celery, pepper, garlic and onions, for 10 minutes.
2 Add the mushrooms, stir and add the potatoes and raisins. Add the tomatoes and stir in the curry powder, salt to taste and soya sauce.
3 Leave the mixture to simmer for 10 minutes then add the tomato purée, stir and simmer for a further 10 minutes. Serve hot with brown rice and salad.

Approximate cost of ingredients: £1.30

● A salad garnish, e.g., watercress or plain cucumber slices can suffice with a meal already containing plenty of vegetables.

> ● Stale bread can be freshened if brushed entirely in milk and baked moderately for 15 minutes. The crust will be crispened and the inside nicer than otherwise.

Bread and Cheese Pudding

Ingredients
12 slices wholemeal bread, spread with margarine
225g/½ lb grated cheese
3 eggs
425ml/¾ pint milk
5ml/1 teaspoon mustard
Salt and freshly ground black pepper
7.5ml/½ tablespoon margarine or butter

Method
1   Make alternate layers of bread and cheese, starting with bread and ending with cheese, in a shallow ovenproof dish. Beat the eggs, milk, mustard and seasoning together and pour over the bread and cheese. Ideally, let stand for 1 hour to 90 minutes. Dot the top with flecks of margarine or butter and bake at 180°C/350°F (Gas Mark 4) for 20 minutes. Serve with salad.

Approximate cost of ingredients: £1.40

Cheese and Tomato Pizza

Ingredients

Base:
115g/4 oz self-raising flour
225g/8 oz plain white flour
170g/6 oz margarine or 45–60ml/3–4 tablespoons vegetable oil
Salt
Water to mix

Top:
2 onions, slice
½ green pepper, sliced
55g/2 oz mushrooms, sliced
2 tomatoes, sliced
225g/8 oz Cheddar, grated
45ml/3 tablespoons tomato purée
Salt and freshly ground black pepper
5ml/1 teaspoon oregano or mixed herbs
Vegetable oil

Method

1　Mix the flours, salt and oil or margarine. Then add water, enough to mix to a stiff dough. Knead until pliable and roll out to ½mm/¼ inch thick. Place in a 18cm/7 inch flan tin.
2　Spread with purée and brush with a little oil.
3　Sprinkle with herbs and place raw vegetables on top starting with the onions and pepper, then mushrooms and tomatoes.
4　Brush with a little vegetable oil and top with the cheese.
5　Bake at 190°C/375°F (Gas Mark 5) in the middle of the oven for 20–25 minutes.

Approximate cost of ingredients: £1.40

Spaghetti Neapolitan

Ingredients
285g/10 oz wholewheat spaghetti
4 small onions, sliced
3 carrots, grated
1 green pepper, chopped
55g/2 oz mushrooms
Crushed garlic, to taste
15–30ml/1–2 tablespoons vegetable oil
395g/14 oz tin tomatoes
15ml/1 tablespoon tomato concentrate
5ml/1 teaspoon mixed dried herbs
15ml/1 tablespoon soya sauce
Salt and freshly ground black pepper

Method
1   Lower the spaghetti into 1.75 litres/3 pints of boiling salted water and cook until soft but not mushy (approximately 12 minutes) then drain.
2   Sauté the vegetables in oil until just tender. Add the tinned tomatoes, tomato concentrate, herbs, soya sauce and seasoning.
3   Cover and cook gently for 30 minutes adding a little more water if the sauce becomes too thick. Serve hot with spaghetti and salad.

Approximate cost of ingredients: £1.53

- Finish off old supplies of food before starting new ones.

Vegetable Pie

Ingredients
225g/½ lb wholemeal self-raising flour
115g/4 oz white plain flour
170g/6 oz margarine
A little milk

Filling:
570ml/1 pint milk
55g/2 oz flour
2 carrots, sliced
115g/4 oz frozen peas
225g/½ lb boiled potatoes, cubed
30–45ml/2–3 tablespoons vegetable oil
Salt and freshly ground black pepper
Milk, for glazing

Method
1   Use the flour and margarine to make crumbly pastry (see page 39). Use three-quarters of the pastry to line a pie dish or tin and keep the rest to make the lid.
2   Stir the milk gradually into the flour, bring to the boil stirring continually until the mixture has thickened to make a white sauce. Set aside.
3   Sauté the vegetables in oil starting with the carrots for 10 minutes. Add the peas and well drained potatoes and cook for a minute.
4   Stir in the sauce, season and use to fill the pie case.
5   Roll out the rest of the pastry to make a lid. Lift on top of the pie, seal the edges and make a small incision in the lid (or prick a few holes with a fork).
6   Brush the top with milk and bake at 170°C/325°F (Gas Mark 3) for 20–25 minutes or until the pastry is cooked. Serve with baked potatoes and salad.

Approximate cost: 95p

Cheese and Vegetable Pie

Ingredients
4 small onions, sliced
15–30ml/1–2 tablespoons vegetable oil
170g/6 oz spinach, rinsed and chopped
455g/1 lb cooked potatoes, sliced or cubed
Kernels from 1 corn on the cob, cooked
115g/4 oz grated Cheddar
570ml/1 pint Medium White Sauce (see page 42)
Salt and freshly ground black pepper

Pastry:
225g/½ lb self-raising wholemeal flour
115g/4 oz white plain flour
170g/6 oz margarine
A little milk

Method
1 Sauté the onions in the oil until golden — about 5 minutes. Stir in the spinach and sauté a further 5 minutes.
2 Add the cooked potatoes and corn kernels. Add the cheese to the sauce and pour this over the vegetables. Stir well and season.
3 Make up the pastry using the flour and margarine and a little milk or water and use half to line a flan case or pie dish. Bake at 170°C/325°F (Gas Mark 3) for 10 minutes.
4 Spoon the vegetables into the case and top with a lid made from the remaining pastry.
5 Brush with milk and bake at 180°C/350°F (Gas Mark 4) on the third rung from the top for 20 minutes until the pastry is golden brown. Serve with baked potatoes and salad.

Approximate cost of ingredients: £1.80

Potato Pie

Ingredients
225g/8 oz streaky bacon
15ml/1 tablespoon vegetable oil
4 small onions or 1 large onion, sliced
30ml/2 tablespoons flour
570ml/1 pint milk
Salt and freshly grated black pepper
Freshly grated nutmeg
680g/1½ lb cooked potatoes, thickly sliced

Pastry:
225g/½ lb self-raising wholemeal flour
115g/4 oz white plain flour
170g/6 oz margarine
A little milk

Method
1 Chop the bacon and fry in the oil. Add the onion and cook until lightly golden.
2 Add the flour, stir well and slowly add the milk. Bring to the boil stirring continually to make a smooth sauce. Season with salt, pepper and nutmeg.
3 Add the cooked potatoes, take off the heat and set aside.
4 Make the pastry using the flour, margarine and a little water to bind the dough. Use half to line a pie dish and bake at 170°C/325°F (Gas Mark 3) for 10 minutes.
5 Spoon in the potato mixture. Cover with a thin lid made from the rest of the pastry. Brush with milk and bake at 180°C/350°F (Gas Mark 4) for 20 minutes until the pastry is golden brown. Serve with Brussels sprouts and salad.

Approximate cost of ingredients: £1.50

• Make a note when supplies of anything are running low. This should help reduce the number of your shopping trips.

Popeye Pasties

Ingredients
285g/10 oz wholemeal flour
140g/5 oz margarine
A little water
3 potatoes, cooked and mashed
285g/10 oz cream cheese
170g/6 oz cooked spinach, chopped
15ml/1 tablespoon chopped chives
45ml/3 tablespoons milk
Salt and freshly ground black pepper
1 small onion, chopped

Method
1   Make pastry from the flour and margarine and a little water (see page 39). With floured hands, shape the pastry into a large roll about 4cm/1½ inches thick. Cut the roll into 12cm/5-inch pieces and roll each one out to a circle. Sprinkle them with flour and leave ready to fill.
2   Combine the potatoes, cream cheese, spinach, chopped chives and milk. Season and add the onion.
3   Put a spoonful of the mixture into the centre of each circle of pastry. Dampen the edges with a little milk, fold the pastries over and press them together so that the filling cannot escape.
4   Brush with milk and bake at 170°C/325°F (Gas Mark 3) for 20 minutes until golden brown. Serve with sour cream or yogurt if liked, baked potatoes and salad.

Approximate cost of ingredients: £1.90

Lentil Flan

(Serves 6)

Ingredients

Pastry:
225g/½ lb wholemeal flour
115g/4 oz margarine
A little cold water or milk

Filling:
250g/9 oz red split lentils
850ml/1½ pints water
4 small onions, sliced
3–4 carrots, grated
Crushed garlic, to taste
15–30ml/1–2 tablespoons vegetable oil
Juice of ½–1 lemon
30ml/2 tablespoons tomato concentrate
Salt and freshly ground black pepper
115g/4 oz grated cheese

Method

1   Make up the pastry by rubbing the fat into the flour and bringing to a dough with a little water. Use to line a flan tin or pie dish and bake at 170°C/325°F (Gas Mark 3) for 10 minutes.

2   Bring the lentils to the boil in the water and simmer, stirring occasionally over a low heat without a lid, for about 15 minutes until soft but not runny (if runny, simmer for a further 10 minutes, stirring continually).

3   Meanwhile, sauté the onion, carrots and garlic in the oil in a covered pan over a low heat for 10–15 minutes.

4   Add the cooked lentils, lemon juice, tomato concentrate and seasoning. Stir well and spoon into the pre-baked pastry case.

5   Bake at 200°C/400°F (Gas Mark 6) for 15 minutes then

sprinkle with the grated cheese and continue to bake at 170°C/325°F (Gas Mark 3) until the cheese has melted. Serve with baked potatoes and salad.

Approximate cost of ingredients: £1.40

- Food not consumed should be stored in the fridge (it will keep for 2 days) and used as soon as possible e.g., quiche will serve re-heated as lunch the following day (waste not want not).

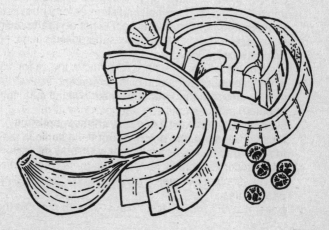

Cowboy Beans

Ingredients
300g/11 oz red kidney beans
1.4 litres/2½ pints water
4 onions, sliced
1 green pepper, sliced
Crushed garlic, to taste
15ml/1 tablespoon vegetable oil
55g/2 oz mushrooms, sliced
395g/14 oz tin tomatoes
10ml/2 teaspoons yeast extract or 30ml/2 tablespoons soya
    sauce
2.5ml–5ml/½–1 teaspoon cayenne pepper
15ml/1 tablespoon tomato purée
Salt

Method
1 Soak the beans overnight and simmer in the water in a
   pan with a tight fitting lid for 90 minutes, or pressure
   cook at 15 lb pressure for 15 minutes. Or, bring the
   unsoaked beans to the boil and simmer for 2½ hours in a
   saucepan with a tight fitting lid. Do not add salt until the
   beans are cooked and use only soft cooked beans —
   see note page 35.
2 Simmer the onions, pepper and garlic in the oil for 10
   minutes over a low heat in a lidded frying pan. Add the
   mushrooms, stir then add the cooked beans and tinned
   tomatoes.
3 Flavour with yeast extract or soya sauce, cayenne
   pepper, tomato purée and salt. Stir then sauté for a
   further 15 minutes. Serve with baked potatoes or rice
   and salad.

Approximate cost of ingredients: £1.45

Variation:

Mexican Beans

Brown 225–455g/½–1 lb mince, add the above vegetables
and sauté as before etc., using the above method.

Approximate cost of ingredients: £3.15

Lentil & Cheese Loaf

Ingredients
145g/5 oz red split lentils
1 pint water
115g/4 oz sage and onion stuffing (dry)
2 carrots, grated
2 medium onions, sliced
Garlic, crushed
2 eggs
115g/4 oz cheese, grated
1–2 oz breadcrumbs
1 tablespoon tomato purée
Salt/freshly ground black pepper

Method
1   Simmer lentils in water for 15 minutes.
2   Sauté vegetables for approximately 15 minutes.
3   Add stuffing to cooked lentils. Mix with the vegetables in
    the frying pan.
4   Season and add cheese and eggs when mixture is quite
    cool.
5   Bake for 20 minutes at 190°C/375°F (Gas Mark 5).
6   Serve with baked potatoes and salad.

Approximate cost of ingredients: £1.30

- Fruit and vegetables are at their best and cheapest when they are in season.

Vegetable Risotto

Ingredients
285g/10 oz brown rice
1.1 litres/2 pints salted water
3 carrots, grated
3 onions, sliced
2 sticks celery, chopped
Crushed garlic, to taste
15–30ml/1–2 tablespoons vegetable oil
115g/4 oz frozen peas
395g/14 oz tin tomatoes
15–30ml/1–2 tablespoons soya sauce
7.5ml/½ tablespoon tomato purée
Salt and freshly ground black pepper

Method
1   Cook the rice in salted water following the recipe on page 34.
2   Whilst the rice is cooking, sauté the carrots, onions, celery and garlic in the oil for 10–15 minutes. Add the peas, tomatoes, stir in the soya sauce and tomato purée.
3   Add the cooked rice and simmer gently for 10 minutes, stirring occasionally. Season to taste. Serve with salad.

Approximate cost of ingredients: £1.35

Sautéed (Stir-Fried) Vegetables

Basically any combination of vegetables can be sautéed but lighter vegetables like mushrooms, sweetcorn, peas and peppers are favoured.

Ingredients
2–3 tablespoons vegetable oil
3 carrots, chopped and sliced lengthways
225g/8 oz courgettes, sliced lengthways
225/8 oz beansprouts
3 tablespoons soya sauce plus ½ pint water *or*
1 tablespoon yeast extract plus ½ pint water
Salt and freshly ground black pepper

Method
1   Start by heating the oil in the pan then add the carrots. Stir, cover and sauté gently for 10 minutes.
2   Add the courgettes, stir and cover, and shortly afterwards add the beansprouts.
3   Stir well, cover and sauté for around 5 minutes before adding the stock. Season to taste, cover and cook for a further 5–10 minutes. Serve with hot rice, etc.

Approximate cost of ingredients: 90p

Fish Pie I

Ingredients
680g/1½ lb filleted fish
10ml/2 teaspoons chopped parsley
1 onion, grated or finely chopped
2 eggs
570ml/1 pint milk
Salt and freshly ground black pepper
30ml/2 tablespoons bread crumbs
55g/2 oz margarine or butter
55g/2 oz grated cheese

Method
1   Poach or sauté the fish, cool, flake and layer into a greased pie dish with the parsley and onion, starting with fish.
2   Beat the eggs, milk and seasoning and pour over the fish.
3   Bake at 180°C/350°F (Gas Mark 4) until the top feels firm. Cover with a mixture of bread crumbs, margarine and cheese. Grill for 3–4 minutes until the cheese is golden brown.
4   Serve with baked potatoes and salad.

Approximate cost of ingredients: £2.26

Fish Pie II

Ingredients
1 corn on the cob
455g/1 lb cooked fish
285ml/$\frac{1}{2}$ pint white sauce
900g/2 lb potato, mashed with a little margarine
Salt and freshly ground black pepper

Method
1   Strip the kernels from the corn and boil in unsalted water
    for 10 minutes. Drain well.
2   Flake the fish into a pie dish. Add the corn. Pour over the
    white sauce.
3   Season the mashed potato and use to cover the pie.
    Bake at 180°C/350°F (Gas Mark 4) for 15 minutes or
    until piping hot.

Approximate cost of ingredients: £1.65

Note:
Use mushrooms or other vegetables when corn is not
available. Serve with lightly-boiled vegetables and salad.

(Can be baked without white sauce, if preferred.)

Baked Mackerel

Ingredients
2 large mackerel (or herring)
30ml/2 tablespoons vegetable oil

Method
1 Brush the cleaned mackerel with oil and place them side by side in an oven-proof dish. Bake on the third rung at 180°C/350°F (Gas Mark 4) for approximately 35 minutes. Alternatively, surround the fish with sliced onion and bake, or stuff cleaned, but unsplit, mackerel with 115g/4 oz of sautéed mushrooms bound with a little flour and seasoned with salt and pepper.
2 Serve with baked potatoes and salad.

Approximate cost of ingredients:£2.00

Spicy Mackerel

Ingredients
285–450ml/½–¾ pints water
1 sprig parsley
15ml/1 tablespoon lemon juice
1 carrot, sliced
1 onion, sliced
Salt and freshly ground black pepper
2 mackerels, filleted (or herring)
30g/1 oz margarine or butter
30g/1 oz flour
5ml/1 teaspoon curry powder

Method

1 Bring the water, parsley, lemon juice, carrot, onion and seasoning slowly to the boil and simmer for 5 minutes.
2 Add the fish and cook gently until tender. Remove the fish and keep warm.
3 Make a sauce by melting the margarine or butter, stirring in the flour and cooking for 1 minute. Slowly add the strained stock and curry powder and stir until smooth and creamy.
4 Return the cooked fish and serve hot with brown rice and salad.

Approximate cost of ingredients: £1.83

Mackerel in Spicy Batter

Ingredients
3 small mackerel, filleted (or herring)

Batter mix:
225g/8 oz self-raising wholemeal flour
5ml/1 teaspoon salt
Pinch cayenne pepper
1 egg
250ml/½ pint milk
approx 90ml/6 tablespoons vegetable oil

Method

1 Mix the dry ingredients, and add the egg. Gradually stir in the milk.
2 Coat the mackerel in the mixture and fry in very hot oil in a cast iron pan, for approximately 5 minutes each side.
3 Keep them hot in the oven until served. (Makes 6 in all).
4 Serve with baked potatoes, peas and salad.

Approximate cost of ingredients: £2.12

Fish Curry

Ingredients
455g/1 lb filleted fish (mackerel or herring)
15ml/1 tablespoon vegetable oil
55g/2 oz margarine or butter
2 onions, chopped
1 eating apple, peeled and chopped
30ml/2 tablespoons flour
285ml/½ pint stock or 5ml/1 teaspoon yeast extract with water
22.5ml/1½ tablespoons curry powder
140ml/¼ pint top of the milk
15ml/1 tablespoon lemon juice
30g/1 oz desiccated coconut
Salt

Method
1   Sauté fish in oil lightly till just tender. Remove them from the pan, add the margarine or butter and fry the onions and apple for a few minutes.
2   Stir in the flour and stock. Stir and add the curry powder and cook for 10 minutes.
3   Pour in the milk, lemon juice, coconut and salt and cook for 2–3 minutes before adding the fish.
4   Simmer gently for 10–12 minutes and serve with brown rice and salad.

Approximate cost of ingredients: £1.55

Fish Cakes

Ingredients
455g/1 lb cooked filleted fish
30–45ml/2–3 tablespoons vegetable oil
900g/2 lb potatoes, cooked
30g/1 oz margarine
5ml/1 teaspoon tomato concentrate
5ml/1 teaspoon yeast extract
2 slices wholemeal bread
1 egg
Salt and freshly ground black pepper
Flour, for shaping

Method
1   Sauté the fish in a little of the oil until flaky.
2   Mash the potatoes and mix with the fish, margarine, tomato concentrate and yeast extract.
3   Grate or blend the bread to make crumbs and add to the mixture with the egg and seasoning.
4   Form into small cakes and roll them in a little flour. Fry the fish cakes on both sides in the remaining oil or bake in a little oil at 200°C/400°F (Gas Mark 6) until crisp and brown.
5   Serve with cauliflower or a suitable vegetable and salad.

Approximate cost of ingredients: £1.50

Macaroni Chicken

Ingredients
225g/½ lb macaroni
1 chicken piece, cooked
2 carrots, grated
2 onions, sliced
Crushed garlic, to taste
115g/4 oz frozen peas
30–45ml/2–3 tablespoons vegetable oil
15ml/1 tablespoon soya sauce
395g/14 oz tin tomatoes
2.5ml/½ teaspoon cayenne pepper
Salt
15ml/1 tablespoon tomato purée

Method
1   Bring 1.75 litres/3 pints of water with 5ml/1 teaspoon salt
    to the boil and add the macaroni. Stir, cover and cook
    until soft but not mushy — about 12 minutes. Drain.
2   Cut the flesh from the cooked chicken into bite-sized
    pieces. Sauté the vegetables in the oil for about 10
    minutes then add the soya sauce, the chicken and the
    tomatoes. Season with cayenne pepper and salt and stir
    in the tomato purée.
3   Cook over a low heat for 1–2 minutes. Add the macaroni
    and cook for a further 5–10 minutes. Serve hot with a
    simple salad.

Approximate cost of ingredients: £2.19

Chicken Casserole

Ingredients
2 chicken quarters
Seasoned flour
30ml/2 tablespoons vegetable oil
900g/2 lb potatoes, chopped
3 carrots, sliced
3 onions, sliced
Crushed garlic, to taste
450–570ml/$\frac{3}{4}$–1 pint hot water with 15ml/3 teaspoons yeast extract
30ml/2 tablespoons fruit juice
7.5ml/$\frac{1}{2}$ tablespoon tomato purée
115g/4 oz frozen peas
Salt and freshly ground black pepper

Method
1   Coat the chicken with seasoned flour and brown in the vegetable oil. Put it into an oven-proof casserole with all the vegetables.
2   Mix the stock and fruit juice with the tomato purée and pour over the vegetables. Bake at 190°C/375°F (Gas Mark 5) for 1 hour.
3   Serve with dumplings.

Approximate cost of ingredients: £2.60

Chicken Fried Rice

Ingredients
330g/11 oz brown rice (see page 34 for cooking instructions)
2 chicken pieces
115g/4 oz frozen peas (from 1kg/2 lb bag)
2 onions, sliced
115g/4 oz finely shredded white cabbage
15–30ml/1–2 tablespoons vegetable oil
60m/4 tablespoons soya sauce
250ml/½ pint hot water
5ml/1 teaspoon miso

Method
1   Heat a little oil in a large frying pan. Sauté chicken for about 20 minutes until cooked. Remove the chicken from the pan, bone and chop.
2   Sauté the cabbage and onion in the pan for 10 minutes. Add the peas and sauté for a further 5 minutes.
3   Add the rice and stir until the grains have separated (about 2–3 minutes).
4   Add the chicken, soya sauce and stock (miso and hot water). Season and stir.
5   Cook to boiling point and serve immediately with Simple Salad.

Approximate cost of ingredients: £2.37

Chicken Curry with Vegetables

Ingredients
2 chicken quarters
1 stick celery, chopped
4 small onions, sliced
Crushed garlic, to taste
1 green pepper, sliced
55g/2 oz mushrooms, sliced
30–45ml/2–3 tablespoons vegetable oil
25ml/5 teaspoons curry powder
395g/14 oz tin tomatoes
30ml/2 tablespoons soya sauce
Salt
15ml/1 tablespoon tomato purée

Method
1   Sauté the chicken until cooked – about 25 minutes. Cool and remove the flesh and cut it into bite-sized pieces.
2   Sauté the vegetables in oil for about 10 minutes. Stir in the curry powder, tinned tomatoes and chicken.
3   Add the soya sauce and salt to taste then simmer for 15 minutes, stirring occasionally.
4   Add the tomato purée and cook for a further 10 minutes. Serve with brown rice and salad.

Approximate cost of ingredients: £3.00

Chicken and Vegetable Pie

Ingredients

1 chicken quarter
4 small onions, sliced
15ml/1 tablespoon vegetable oil
1 corn on the cob (substitute carrots when corn is not
  available)
170g/6 oz spinach, rinsed and chopped
570ml/1 pint medium white sauce
Salt and freshly ground black pepper

Pastry:
340g/¾ lb wholemeal self-raising flour
170g/6 oz margarine
A little milk

Method

1   Fry the chicken until cooked, about 30 minutes. Cook, remove the flesh and cut into bite-sized pieces.
2   Sauté the onions in the vegetable oil for about 5 minutes. Cut the corn kernels from the cob and add them to the onion. Stir well and add the spinach.
3   Stir fry for a further 5 minutes then add to the chicken and white sauce. Stir well and season to taste.
4   Make up the pastry from the flour and margarine bound with a little water and use half to line a flan case or pie plate. Bake at 170°C/325°F (Gas Mark 3) for 10 minutes.
5   Fill with the chicken mixture and cover with a lid made from the remaining pastry. Make a small slit in the centre of the lid, brush all over with milk and continue to bake at 180°C/350°F (Gas Mark 4) for 20 minutes until the pastry is golden brown. Serve with baked potatoes and salad.

Approximate cost of ingredients: £2.35

Spicy Spare Rib Chops

Ingredients

Sauce:
10ml/2 teaspoons salt
30ml/2 tablespoons sugar
15ml/1 tablespoon vinegar
30ml/2 tablespoons soya sauce
150ml/5 fl oz apple juice
2.5ml/$\frac{1}{2}$ teaspoon cayenne pepper
680g/1$\frac{1}{2}$ lb spare rib chops, cut large
15ml/1 tablespoon wholemeal flour

Method

1   Mix the sauce ingredients together in a heavy-based saucepan or casserole. Add 285ml/$\frac{1}{2}$ pint water, stir.
2   Cut the chops into large pieces and add to the sauce. Bring to the boil, cover and simmer gently for about 45 minutes turning the pieces occasionally.
3   When the meat is tender, sprinkle the flour into the sauce, stirring continually until the sauce thickens. Serve with rice or spaghetti.

Approximate cost of ingredients: £2.20

● To remove grease from soup or gravy dip in small pieces of clean tissue to absorb the fat.

Pork and Beans

Ingredients
130/5 oz blackeye beans
500ml/1 pint water
680g/1½ lb spare rib pork chops
1 large onion, sliced
Crushed garlic, to taste
15ml/1 tablespoon vegetable oil
30ml/2 tablespoons soya sauce
Sea salt and freshly ground black pepper
5ml/1 teaspoon brown sugar
5ml/1 teaspoon vinegar
395g/14 oz tin tomatoes

Method
1 Boil the beans in the water until cooked — about 25–30 minutes.
2 Fry the chops lightly on both sides.
3 Add the onion and garlic with the oil if needed and fry until the onions are golden.
4 Add the beans with their water, the tomatoes and the rest of the ingredients. Cook for a further 5 minutes then turn the mixture into a deep oven-proof casserole.
5 Cover and bake at 190°C/375°F (Gas Mark 5) for about 1 hour. Serve with potatoes or rice and salad.

Approximate cost of ingredients: £2.70

Kidney and Bacon Pilaff

Ingredients
285g/10 oz brown rice
1.1 litres/2 pints salted water
340g/¾ lb lamb's kidneys, chopped in half
115g/4 oz streaky bacon
1 large onion, sliced
115g/4 oz mushrooms, sliced
285ml/½ pint stock or water with 5ml/1 teaspoon yeast
extract 15ml/1 tablespoon wholemeal flour
15–30ml/1–2 tablespoons vegetable oil

Method
1   Cook the rice in salted water following the recipe on
    page 34.
2   Fry bacon till quite crisp. Add the kidneys and fry for
    5–10 minutes, stirring occasionally. Add onions and
    cover. Sauté for 5 minutes and add mushrooms.
3   Sauté for 1 minute and stir in the stock and simmer until
    ingredients are tender. Kidney and bacon may be
    removed at this stage and chopped.
4   Return to the pan, sprinkle on the flour and stir into the
    pilaff continually over a moderate heat, until the sauce
    thickens. Serve with a border of rice and a salad.

Approximate cost of ingredients: £2.10

- Make a mock beef stock out of a little onion, carrot,
  celery, grated garlic and soya sauce. Simply
  simmer for 10 minutes.

Rice with Mince

Ingredients
285g/10 oz brown rice
1.1litres/2 pints salted water
225g/8 oz minced lamb
15–30ml/1–2 tablespoons vegetable oil
3 onions, sliced
Crushed garlic, to taste
Finely chopped parsley
Salt and freshly ground black pepper

Method
1   Cook the rice in the salted water following the recipe on page 34.
2   Brown the mince in hot oil. Add the onion and garlic and sauté for 5 minutes.
3. Add the parsley and sauté for a further 5–10 minutes. Add the cooked rice, stir and season. Serve with tomato sauce (page 43) and salad.

Approximate cost of ingredients: £1.60

Liver and Mushrooms I

Ingredients
1 large onion, sliced
30ml/2 tablespoons vegetable oil
115g/4 oz mushrooms, sliced
455g/1 lb liver of choice, chopped small and rolled in flour
2.5ml/½ teaspoon marjoram
Salt and freshly ground black pepper
285ml/½ pint stock or water mixed with 5ml/1 teaspoon yeast extract

Method
1 Fry the onion in the oil until golden. Add the mushrooms and liver and fry slowly for 5 minutes.
2 Sprinkle with majoram and season to taste. Pour on the stock and cook over a low heat until the liver is tender. Serve with wholewheat macaroni or noodles.

Approximate cost of ingredients: £1.44

Liver and Mushrooms II

Ingredients
Crushed garlic, to taste
15–30ml/1–2 tablespoons vegetable oil
455g/1 lb lamb's liver of choice, thinly sliced
Freshly ground black pepper
115g/4 oz mushrooms, sliced

Method
1 Sauté the garlic in oil for 5 minutes. Add the liver and sprinkle liberally with black pepper.
2 Prick the liver with a fork and fry gently on both sides for about 10 minutes.
3 Add the mushrooms, stir and cover. Continue to cook gently for a further 5 minutes. Serve with potatoes or rice and salad.

Approximate cost of ingredients: £1.50

Baked Liver and Bacon

Ingredients
15–30ml/1–2 tablespoons vegetable oil
455g/1 lb thinly sliced liver of choice
8 rashers streaky bacon

Method
1   Grease a shallow baking dish with the oil and coat liver on both sides with the oil. Arrange liver in dish and place the bacon on top.
2   Bake in a moderate oven 180°C/350°F (Gas Mark 4) until bacon is crisp, approximately 15–20 minutes. Serve with baked potatoes and salad.

Approximate cost of ingredients: £1.50

Liver and Bacon Casserole

Ingredients

455g/1 lb lamb's liver
225/½ lb streaky bacon (from 1kg/2 lb bag bacon pieces)
3 onions, sliced
5ml/1 tablespoon tomato purée
250–425ml/½–¾ pint hot water
Salt/freshly ground black pepper
30–45ml/2–3 tablespoons wholemeal flour, salt/pepper and mixed herbs

Method

1 Put the flour, salt, pepper and herbs in a small plastic bag along with the thinly sliced liver.
2 Shake until the liver and flour are well mixed.
3 Place the coated liver in a greased enamel, cast-iron casserole and top with the bacon.
4 Place in a hot oven on the top shelf (200°C/400°F/Gas Mark 6) and let the bacon crisp without the casserole lid for 20 minutes.
5 Place the onions on top and pour on the stock (yeast extract and tomato purée dissolved in the hot water).
6 Cover and bake for a further 15–20 minutes.
7 Serve with sprouts and baked potatoes.

Approximate cost of ingredients: £1.90

Spaghetti Joe

Ingredients
170g/6 oz shoulder ham, in one piece
115g/4 oz mushrooms, sliced
340g/12 oz wholewheat spaghetti
15ml/1 tablespoon oil

Tomato sauce:
3 onions, sliced
3 sticks celery, chopped
395g/14 oz tin tomatoes
10ml/2 teaspoons demerara sugar
5ml/1 teaspoon yeast extract or 10ml/2 tablespoons soya
    sauce
15ml/1 tablespoon oil

Method
1   Sauté onion and celery in oil for 10 minutes, then place in
    saucepan with tinned tomatoes. Add the sugar and soya
    sauce, and season with salt and freshly ground black
    pepper.
2   Meanwhile, add the spaghetti to a large pan of boiling,
    salted water. Boil until quite tender, approximately 10
    minutes, then drain.
3   Cut the ham into strips and sauté lightly with mushrooms
    in vegetable oil for 5 minutes.
4   Fold in the spaghetti and toss until well glazed.
5   Serve hot with tomato sauce and simple salad.

Approximate cost of ingredients: £2.25

Roast Chicken

Ingredients
1 roasting chicken without giblets
115g/4 oz sage and onion stuffing (made up)

Baste:
1 teaspoon salt
2 teaspoons soya sauce
½ teaspoon sugar
1 teaspoon vinegar
2 teaspoons vegetable oil

Method
1   Place the chicken in a roasting tin. Remove any surplus fat from leg cavity and fill with the sage and onion stuffing.
2   Mix the baste ingredients, adding the oil last, and brush the chicken all over with it. Bake at 200°C/400°F (Gas Mark 6) on the third rung from the top for approximately 1 hour 15 minutes, till the juices burst and the fat runs and the skin is browned and crispy.

Approximate cost of ingredients: £3.50

Note:
To avoid the spread of food poisoning care must be taken to make sure that uncooked chicken is well wrapped when stored in the refrigerator and not directly in contact with other food. Also, any worktops used for preparing chicken must be washed down thoroughly.

• The bones left over from a chicken or Christmas turkey make excellent stock. Simply boil with any left-over bits of vegetables i.e., carrots, onions, celery etc., for about 25 minutes.

5
Salads

Green Salad

Ingredients
½ lettuce
½ bunch watercress
Cucumber, sliced
½ green pepper, sliced
Small spring onion, finely chopped
A few green olives

Method
1 Rinse and drain the lettuce and watercress. Chop the lettuce and add other ingredients.
2 Top with a simple dressing of 5ml/1 teaspoon salt, vinegar and oil mixed in an egg cup and with a liberal sprinkling of freshly ground pepper.

Approximate cost: 75p

- Sad and limp watercress can be revived by standing upright in cold water.

Orange and Onion Salad

Ingredients
3 oranges
3 onions, chopped

Dressing:
15ml/1 tablespoon vegetable oil
10ml/2 teaspoons vinegar
5ml/1 teaspoon lemon juice
2.5ml/$\frac{1}{2}$ teaspoon chopped tarragon
2.5ml/$\frac{1}{2}$ teaspoon sugar

Method
1   Peel the oranges removing white pith. Slice into rounds,
    removing the seeds.
2   Combine with the onions and add the salad dressing.

Approximate cost: 60p

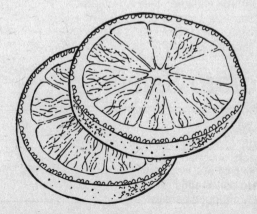

Rice Salad

Ingredients
300g/11 oz brown rice
2 carrots, grated
115g/4 oz white cabbage, shredded
1 small onion, minced
115g/4 oz cooked green peas
15ml/1 tablespoon raisins

Dressing:
5ml/1 teaspoon salt
15ml/1 tablespoon soya sauce
15ml/1 tablespoon vinegar
2.5ml/½ teaspoon mustard powder
15ml/1 tablespoon vegetable oil

Method
1   Boil the rice until tender but not mushy (see page 34).
2   Add the other ingredients to hot rice and season with the mixed dressing. Serve hot or cold.

Approximate cost: 85p

Potato Salad

Ingredients
900g/2 lb potatoes, cooked and cubed
1 onion, chopped
2 stalks celery, chopped
2 hard boiled eggs, sliced
Finely chopped parsley

Dressing:
115g/4 oz cream cheese
15ml/1 tablespoon vegetable oil
15ml/1 tablespoon vinegar
Salt and freshly ground black pepper

Method
1 Cook the potatoes until just tender but not soft. Cube and combine with the remaining ingredients whilst hot, adding the salad dressing last.
2 Chill and serve.

Approximate cost: £1.06p

Redbean Salad

Ingredients
300g/11 oz red kidney beans
1 green pepper, chopped
2 stalks celery, chopped
1 onion, finely chopped
Crushed garlic, to taste

Dressing:
15ml/1 tablespoon lemon juice
15ml/1 tablespoon vegetable oil
Salt and freshly ground black pepper

Method
1 Cook the beans as outlined on page 35.
2 Mix all the ingredients together with the dressing ingredients, whilst the beans are still hot. Chill and serve.

Approximate cost: £1.05p

Curried Rice Salad

Ingredients
300g/11 oz brown rice
1 green pepper, chopped
2 sticks celery
2 carrots, grated
1 small onion, chopped finely
1 small apple, grated

Dressing:
5ml/1 teaspoon salt,
15ml/1 tablespoon soya sauce
15ml/1 tablespoon vinegar
10–15ml/2–3 teaspoons curry powder
15ml/1 tablespoon vegetable oil

Method
1   Boil the rice until soft but not mushy.
2   Add ingredients to hot rice and season with the dressing.
    Serve hot or cold.

Approximate cost: £1.30

Macaroni Salad

Ingredients
225g/½ lb macaroni
115g/4 oz cooked peas or sweet corn
55g/2 oz mushrooms, sliced
2 stalks celery chopped
Finely chopped parsley

Dressing:
150g/5 oz carton natural yogurt
15ml/1 tablespoon vegetable oil
15ml/1 tablespoon orange juice
Salt and freshly ground black pepper

Method
1 Cook macaroni as outlined on page 106. Combine with the rest of the ingredients and the dressing whilst the macaroni is hot.
2 Chill and serve. Alternatively add tinned tuna (drained) to the ingredients when cold.

Approximate cost: 98p

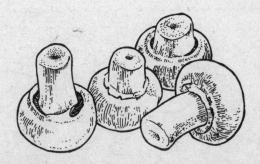

Mackerel Salad

Ingredients
1 medium mackerel
½ round lettuce, rinsed
½ bunch watercress, rinsed and chopped
1 onion, finely chopped
1 carrot, grated
Piece cucumber, sliced
A few olives

Dressing:
15ml/1 tablespoon lemon juice
5ml/1 teaspoon mustard powder
15ml/1 tablespoon vegetable oil
Salt and freshly ground black pepper

Method
1   If not using filleted fish, bake in a moderate oven
    preheated to 180°C/350°F (Gas Mark 4) for about 20
    minutes and remove bones. If filleted sauté till flaky.
2   Marinate for up to 1 hour in the dressing then add other
    ingredients and mix well.

Approximate cost: £1.63

Chicken Salad

Ingredients
2 pieces chicken, cooked
2 carrots, grated
½ green pepper
2 stalks celery, chopped
Piece cucumber, sliced
Few mushrooms, sliced
A tomato, sliced
A few raisins

Dressing:
150g/5 oz carton natural yogurt
60ml/4 tablespoons top of the milk
5ml/1 teaspoon lemon juice
15ml/1 tablespoon vegetable oil
Salt and freshly ground black pepper

Method
1   If not using cooked chicken, sauté chicken for about 30
    minutes in a covered pan, turning occasionally.
2   Remove meat from the bone and marinate for up to 1
    hour in a mixed dressing of 5ml/1 teaspoon salt, 2.5ml/½
    teaspoon black pepper, 2.5ml/½ teaspoon mustard
    powder, 2.5ml/½ teaspoon sugar, 15ml/1 tablespoon
    lemon juice or vinegar and 10ml/2 teaspoons oil.
3   Drain if necessary and combine with other ingredients,
    plus the yogurt dressing.

Approximate cost: £2.88

● Do not buy more food than can be used while it is
  still in first class condition. Green vegetables and
  perishables should be bought fresh daily.

Winter Salad

Ingredients
225g/½ lb red cabbage, finely shredded
2 carrots, grated
2 sticks green celery, sliced
1 small apple, grated
½ onion, sliced
1 tablespoon raisins
Oil and vinegar, yogurt or cream cheese dressing

Method
Mix together all the ingredients and serve with the dressing
of your choice.

Approximate cost of ingredients: 55p

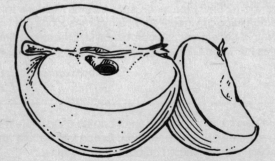

6
Desserts

Bread and Butter Pudding

Ingredients
6 slices wholemeal bread, spread with margarine
115g/4 oz sultanas
2 eggs
55g/2 oz brown sugar
570ml/1 pint milk

Method
1   Arrange layers of bread and sultanas, ending with a layer of bread, in a greased, oven-proof pie dish (bread should only half fill the dish).
2   Beat the eggs, sugar and milk and pour over the bread.
3   Bake at 180°C/350°F (Gas Mark 4) for 1 hour.

Approximate cost of ingredients: £1.00

Humble Crumble

Ingredients
455g/1 lb cooking apples, plums or rhubarb
15ml/1 tablespoon demerara sugar
150–300ml/5–10 fl oz water
115g/4 oz margarine
170g/6 oz wholemeal flour
170g/6 oz porridge oats
85g/3 oz demerara sugar
15ml/1 tablespoon vegetable oil

Method
1   Rinse, quarter and core the apples. Slice them into a shallow oven-proof dish, packing the slices in tightly.
2   Sprinkle with 15ml/1 tablespoon sugar and add the water.
3   Make a crumble topping by rubbing the fat into the dry ingredients. Add a little oil if the mixture still feels dry after mixing. Spoon the crumble over the fruit and bake at 190°C/375°F (Gas Mark 5) for 25–30 minutes or until the fruit starts to bubble up and the crumble topping turns brown. Serve with custard, cream, ice cream, or yogurt.

Approximate cost of ingredients: 89p

Fruity Pie

Ingredients
Pastry:
225g/½ lb self-raising wholemeal flour
115g/4 oz plain white flour
170g/6 oz margarine
A little milk or water

Filling:
455g/1 lb cooking apples
30ml/2 tablespoons demerara sugar
30–450ml/2–3 tablespoons water

Method
1   Make the pastry using the method outlined in Basic
    Essentials (page 39). Use three-quarters of the pastry to
    line an oven-proof pie dish and bake blind at 170°C/
    325°F (Gas Mark 3) for 8–10 minutes.
2   For the filling, rinse, quarter and core the apples. Slice
    them into the pastry-lined dish, sprinkle them with sugar
    and add the water.
3   Cover with a lid made from the remaining pastry. Make a
    small hole in the centre and brush the pastry with milk.
4   Bake on the middle shelf of the oven at 180°C/350°F
    (Gas Mark 4) for 30 minutes until the pastry is golden
    brown and the fruit well cooked. Serve with custard,
    cream, ice cream or yogurt.

Approximate cost of ingredients: 88p

Note:
The following combinations make good fruit pies: blackberry
and apple, apple and raisins with cinnamon, rhubarb and
lemon, apple, gooseberry and banana.

Wholefruit Cake

Ingredients
170g/6 oz demerara sugar
85g/3 oz margarine
455g/1 lb dried fruit
5ml/1 teaspoon mixed spice
5ml/1 level teaspoon bicarbonate of soda
570ml/1 pint water
2 eggs
455g/1 lb self-raising wholemeal flour

Method
1   Put all the ingredients except the eggs and flour, into a saucepan. Add the 570ml/1 pint water and bring to the boil. Turn off the heat, stir and cover. Leave to cool for 1 hour.
2   When cool, beat in the eggs and gradually stir in the flour.
3   Turn into a greased 25cm/10-inch tin and bake at 170°C/325°F (Gas Mark 3) for 1½–2 hours or until a knife inserted into the middle comes out clean.

Approximate cost of ingredients: £1.40

Note:
This recipe doubles as a party cake with the addition of lemon icing made with lemon juice and icing sugar and topped with glacé cherries.

- To freshen stale cake put the cake in a pudding basin, cover with a lid or plate and steam for 30 minutes.

Flapjacks

Ingredients
140g/5 oz margarine
85g/3 oz demerara sugar
15ml/1 tablespoon molasses or black treacle
225g/8 oz rolled oats

Method
1   Melt the margarine, sugar and molasses slowly in a large saucepan. Add the oats and spread onto an oiled, shallow 25cm/10-inch round baking tin and bake at 190°C/375°F (Gas Mark 5) for 20–25 minutes.
2   Mark into squares while still hot and remove from the tin when cold.

Approximate cost of ingredients: 57p

Wholemeal Scones

Ingredients
680g/1½ lb wholemeal flour
5ml/1 rounded teaspoon baking powder
2.5ml/½ teaspoon salt
200g/7 oz margarine
200g/7 oz sultanas
570ml/1 pint milk and water mixed
Beaten egg, to glaze

Method
1   Mix the flour, baking powder and salt. Rub in the margarine until the mixture is like breadcrumbs.
2   Add the sultanas and the milk mixture and stir to make a soft dough. Knead lightly on a floured surface to make a ball then roll out to 2cm/¾ inch thick and cut out about 10 rounds.
3   Transfer them to a greased baking tray, brush with beaten egg and bake at 180°C/350°F (Gas Mark 4) for 20 minutes.

Approximate cost of ingredients: £1.21

Oat Cookies

Ingredients
115g/4 oz margarine
85g/3 oz demerara sugar
115g/4 oz crunchy peanut butter
115g/4 oz oats
115g/4 oz self-raising wholemeal flour
55g/2 oz raisins
5ml/1 teaspoon bicarbonate of soda

Method
1   Melt the margarine and sugar in a saucepan. Stir in the peanut butter, oats, flour, raisins and bicarbonate of soda and mix well.
2   Place spoonfuls of the mixture onto a greased baking sheet. Bake in the middle of the oven at 180°C/350°F (Gas Mark 4) for 20 minutes.

Approximate cost of ingredients: 78p

Potato Cheesecake

Ingredients

Base:
115g/4 oz self-raising wholemeal flour
170g/6 oz plain white flour
55g/2 oz demerara sugar
115g/4 oz butter or margarine
30ml/2 tablespoons vegetable oil

Filling:
55g/2 oz butter or margarine
115g/4 oz demerara sugar
115g/4 oz sultanas
680g/1½ lb mashed potato
Squirt lemon juice

Method

1   Mix together the flours and the sugar and rub in the fat.
    Add oil and a little water to mix to a dough. Line a
    18–20cm/7''–8'' flan tin and bake for approximately 7
    minutes at 180°–190°C/350°C–375°F (Gas Mark 4–5).
2   Beat the butter and sugar together until creamy. Stir in
    the eggs and fold in the dried fruit, mashed potato and
    lemon juice.
3   Spread the mixture onto the flan base and bake for
    approximately 1 hour, oven temperature as before, until
    set and golden brown.

                    Approximate cost of ingredients: £1.40

Exemplary Menus for 4 Weeks

It may be helpful at this point to explain that should you overshoot the weekly figure of £35 in the initial weeks, this need not mean a failure to budget successfully. If, for example, in the first week you should decide on Mulligatawny Soup for Wednesday's lunch, which entails purchase of a pack of cayenne pepper for 50p, only to use a penny's worth, you'll not need to buy any more cayenne pepper for a month of Sundays, and your weekly budget will gradually balance out.

A good way to keep within budget is to use up any ingredients you may already have in, for example, if you have plenty of carrots, lettuce, tomato and cucumber and about 340g/¾ lb of lentils, you could make a Lentil Flan. You would only need to buy onions, garlic, lemon, watercress and potatoes to make Lentil Flan with baked potatoes and Simple Salad.

- Shopping is easier if menus are planned several days or a week in advance.

> ● The purchase of concentrated fruit juice proves convenient as it takes up less space in your fridge than bulky cartons (1 litre easily serves our family for a week), and carton juice is usually made from concentrated juice.

Week One

	Breakfasts	Lunches	Dinners	Total
Sun	Miser's Muesli for 4, 80p	Mackerel Pâté 12 slices wholemeal bread 85p	Roast Chicken Baked Potatoes Salad £4.10	£5.75
Mon	Boiled eggs and wholemeal toast (8 slices) 60p	Sardines on toast (12 slices) £1.32	Lentil Flan Baked Potatoes Salad £2.20	£4.12
Tue	Boiled eggs and wholemeal toast 60p	Baked beans (1 lb 4 oz/567g tin) wholemeal toast (8 slices) 74p	Spaghetti Neapolitan Salad £2.13	£3.47
Wed	Boiled eggs and wholemeal toast 60p	Cream Mushroom Soup, wholemeal bread £1.14	Blackeye Beanburgers Baked Potatoes Salad £1.88	£3.62
Thu	Cornmeal Pudding 52p	Pilchards on toast (12 slices) 84p	Mexican Beans Baked Potatoes Salad £3.80	£5.16
Fri	Oat Porridge 50p	Humous Spread on wholemeal bread (12 slices) with salad 80p	Spicy Mackerel Brown rice Salad £2.83	£4.13
Sat	Boiled eggs and wholemeal toast 60p	Sweet Pancakes with honey/lemon/banana 86p	Cheese & Vegetable Pie Baked Potatoes Salad £2.60	£4.06
				£30.31

Week Two

	Breakfasts	Lunches	Dinners	Total
Sun	4 boiled eggs, toast (8 slices) 60p	Redbean Salad bread (8 slices) £1.29	Chicken Curry Boiled Rice Salad £3.95	£5.84
Mon	Oat Porridge for 4 50p	Lentil Soup, bread, £1.32	Popeye Pasties Baked Potatoes Salad £2.65	£4.47
Tue	Oat Porridge 50p	Cheese Omelette, wholemeal bread 98p	Quick Quiche Baked Potatoes Salad £2.15	£3.63
Wed	Oat Porridge 50p	Humous Spread on bread (12 slices) 80p	Potato Pie Salad £2.10	£3.40
Thu	Oat Porridge 50p	Cream Mushroom Soup, wholemeal bread (8 slices) £1.14	Spaghetti Neopolitan Salad £2.13	£3.77
Fri	Oat Porridge 50p	Mushroom, Onion and Beansprout Pancakes £1.10	Baked Mackerel Baked potatoes Salad £2.80	£4.40
Sat	Boiled eggs and wholemeal toast 48p	Macaroni Salad wholemeal bread (4 slices) £1.10	Cowboy Beans Baked Potatoes Salad £2.25	£3.95
				£29.46

Week Three

	Breakfasts	Lunches	Dinners	Total
Sun	4 boiled eggs 8 slices wholemeal toast 60p	Mackerel Salad £1.63	Chicken & Vegetable Pie Baked Potatoes Salad £3.15	£5.38
Mon	Cornmeal Porridge for 4 73p	Cream Cheese and Spinach Pancakes £1.44	Redbean Burgers Baked Potatoes Salad £1.95	£4.15
Tue	Cornmeal Porridge 73p	Minestrone Soup wholemeal bread 94p	Fish Curry Salad £2.60	£4.27
Wed	Cornmeal Pudding 52p	Yorkshire Omelette wholemeal bread £1.14	Pizza Baked Potatoes Salad £2.20	£3.86

	Breakfasts	Lunches	Dinners	Total
Thu	Cornmeal Porridge **73p**	Mushroom Onion and Beansprout Pancakes **£1.10**	Spring Vegetable Soup wholemeal bread (8 slices) Humble Crumble Custard **£2.34**	**£4.17**
Fri	Cornmeal Porridge **73p**	Baked beans (1lb 4 oz/ 567g tin), wholemeal toast **74p**	Spaghetti Bolognaise Salad **£2.85**	**£4.32**
Sat	4 boiled eggs and wholemeal toast (8 slices) **60p**	Redbean Salad wholemeal bread **£1.30**	Lentil Flan Baked Potatoes Salad **£2.20**	**£4.10**
				£30.32

Week Four

	Breakfasts	Lunches	Dinners	Total
Sun	4 boiled eggs and wholemeal toast (8 slices) **60p**	Taramasalata wholemeal bread (12 slices) salad **90p**	Roast Chicken Baked Potatoes Salad **£4.10**	**£5.60**
Mon	Miser's Muesli **80p**	Cream Celery Soup wholemeal bread (8 slices) **£1.18**	Blackeye Beanburgers Baked Potatoes Salad **£2.10**	**£4.08**
Tue	Miser's Muesli **80p**	Baked beans wholemeal toast (8 slices) **74p**	Lentil and Cheese Loaf Baked Potatoes Salad **£2.10**	**£3.64**
Wed	Miser's Muesli **80p**	Tomato Bouillon wholemeal bread (8 slices) **94p**	Baked Mackerel Baked Potatoes Salad **£2.80**	**£4.54**
Thu	Miser's Muesli **80p**	Welsh Rarebit wholemeal toast (12 slices) **£1.42**	Vegetable Curry Brown Rice Salad **£2.33**	**£4.55**
Fri	Toast Cereal **48p**	Pilchards on toast (12 slices), **76p**	Quick Quiche Baked Potatoes Salad **£2.15**	**£3.39**
Sat	Bread Cereal **72p**	Sweet Pancakes with honey/lemon/banana, **94p**	Fish Cakes Baked Potatoes Salad **£2.30**	**£3.96**
				£29.76

Index